What Every T Know About Laws and Regulations

Myrna Mandlawitz

MRM Associates, Legislative and Consulting Services

PEARSON

Boston   New York   San Francisco
Mexico City   Montreal   Toronto   London   Madrid   Munich   Paris
Hong Kong   Singapore   Tokyo   Cape Town   Sydney

Executive Editor: Virginia Lanigan
Marketing Manager: Kris Ellis-Levy

ISBN: 0-205-50568-6

Printed in the United States of America

10   9   8   7   6   5   4   3   2   1   10   09   08   07   06

Table of Contents

Part C: Infants and Toddlers with Disabilities   130

Part D: National Activities to Improve Education of Children with Disabilities   132

INTRODUCTION: How This Book Is Organized

The new IDEA regulations, issued on August 14, 2006, implement the amendments to the IDEA passed by Congress in the *Individuals with Disabilities Education Improvement Act,* P.L. 108-446 (Dec. 3, 2004). In designing these latest regulations, the U.S. Department of Education decided to include much of the new statutory language *within* the body of the regulations themselves, thus allowing interested individuals to find both the law and regulations in one comprehensive document.

Therefore, in keeping with the Department of Education's intent that virtually "all you need to know" about IDEA be found within the regulations document, this book also highlights both the statutory and the regulatory changes together. Citations generally are to the regulatory sections, and the organization of the text also follows the sequence of the regulations. In the few instances where there are no accompanying regulations for new statutory changes, citations are to the statutory sections and are noted as such. As an additional help for the reader in locating particular topics and terms of interest, a full index is provided at the back of the book.

How to read this document: Information under the heading "2006 Regulations" provides the changes, additions, and deletions from the 1999 Regulations. Unless noted, the information under the heading "1999 Regulations" has been carried over into the 2006 regulations, with the changes noted in the 2006 column.

PART A—General

Definitions Used in the Act [Regulatory Secs. 300.4–300.45; Statutory Sec. 602]

Several new definitions have been added to the IDEA, reflecting the continuing evolution of the law and the desire to align the IDEA with the Elementary and Secondary Education Act (Currently known as the No Child Left Behind Act of 2001, or NCLB).

1999 Regulations (IDEA '97, P.L. 105-17)	2006 Regulations (IDEA '04, P.L. 108-446)
Sec. 300.5. "Assistive Technology Device." Any item, equipment, or product used to increase, maintain, or improve functional capabilities.	*Sec. 300.5. "Assistive Technology Device."* Adds that the term does not include surgically implanted medical device or replacement of such a device.

"Assistive Technology Device." This exception arose in part from a concern, heightened by several due process hearings, that school districts might be held responsible for provision of cochlear implants for children with hearing impairments. See also, "Related Services," Sec. 300.34.

Sec. 300.6. "Assistive Technology Service." Services that directly assist children in the selection, acquisition, or use of assistive technology devices.	*Sec. 300.6. "Assistive Technology Service."* Provision has not changed.

"Charter School." No comparable language.	*Sec. 300.7. "Charter School."* Adds NCLB definition [Sec. 5210(1)]—A charter school is a public school, operating under State statute, which exempts it from certain State or local

1

1999 Regulations (IDEA '97, P.L. 105-17)	2006 Regulations (IDEA '04, P.L. 108-446)
	rules that would inhibit flexible operation and management and which has a performance contract with the public chartering agency that describes how student performance will be measured.
Sec. 300.7. "Child with a Disability." 1. A "child with a disability" is a child evaluated (Secs. 300.304–300.311) as having mental retardation, hearing impairment (including deafness), speech or language impairment, visual impairment (including blindness), serious emotional disturbance, orthopedic impairment, autism, traumatic brain injury, other health impairment, specific learning disability, deaf-blindness, or multiple disabilities, and who, due to the disability, needs special education and related services. 2. SEAs and LEAs may, at their discretion, include children ages 3–9 experiencing developmental delays in physical, cognitive, communication, social or emotional, or adaptive development, and who, because of the delay, need special education and related services. 3. Definitions of disability terms: a. Autism: developmental disability significantly affecting verbal and nonverbal communication and social interaction; term not applicable if performance is affected mainly due to an emotional disturbance.	***Sec. 300.8. "Child with a Disability."*** These definitions generally remain the same, with the following changes: 1. Developmental delay: States may use any subset of the age range of 3 through 9, including ages 3 through 5. 2. Other health impairment: "Tourette syndrome" is added to the list of chronic or acute health problems.

2

b. Deaf-blindness: concomitant hearing and visual impairments causing severe communication and other developmental and educational needs.

c. Deafness: hearing impairment that is so severe as to cause impaired processing of linguistic information through hearing.

d. Emotional disturbance: exhibiting one or more of the following over a long period of time and to a marked degree— inability to learn not explained by intellectual, sensory, or health factors; inability to maintain satisfactory interpersonal relationships; inappropriate behaviors; pervasive unhappiness or depression; or physical symptoms or fears associated with personal or school problems.

e. Hearing impairment: impairment in hearing that affects educational performance, but not included under definition of "deafness."

f. Mental retardation: significantly subaverage general intellectual functioning, with deficits in adaptive behavior.

g. Multiple disabilities: co-occurring impairments, causing severe educational needs; does not include deaf-blindness.

h. Orthopedic impairment: severe orthopedic impairment, including impairments caused by

3

congenital anomaly, disease, and other causes.

i. Other health impairment: limited strength, vitality, or alertness resulting in limited alertness in the educational environment attributable to chronic or acute health problems, such as asthma, ADD/ADHD, diabetes, epilepsy, heart condition, hemophilia, lead poisoning, leukemia, nephritis, rheumatic fever, and sickle cell anemia.

j. Specific learning disability: disorder in one or more psychological processes involved in understanding or using spoken or written language, that may be manifest as an imperfect ability to listen, think, speak, read, write, spell, or do math; does not include learning problems primarily resulting from visual, hearing, or motor disabilities, mental retardation, emotional disturbance, or environmental, cultural, or economic factors.

k. Speech or language impairment: communication disorders, or language or voice impairments.

l. Traumatic brain injury: acquired injury to the brain caused by external physical force resulting in total or partial functional disability or psychosocial impairment, or both.

m. Visual impairment: vision impairment including partial sight and blindness.

"Child with a Disability: Other Health Impairment." The list of "other health impairments" is not exhaustive. Children with Tourette syndrome are often misclassified as having emotional or behavioral problems, when, in fact, Tourette syndrome is a neurological disorder. This addition was made to address misclassification and to ensure that children are appropriately served.

1999 Regulations (IDEA '97, P.L. 105-17)	2006 Regulations (IDEA '04, P.L. 108-446)
Sec. 300.8. "Consent." 1. Regarding the activity for which consent is sought, parents (a) have been fully informed, in their native language or other mode of communication; (b) understand and agree in writing to the activity, and the consent includes a description of the activity and lists records, if any, that will be released and to whom; and, (c) understand that consent is voluntary and may be revoked at any time. 2. If parents revoke consent, revocation is not retroactive, i.e., actions occurring after consent but before revocation are not negated by revoking consent.	*Sec. 300.9. "Consent."* Provision has not changed.
"Core Academic Subjects." No comparable language.	*Sec. 300.10. "Core Academic Subjects."* Adds NCLB definition [Sec. 9101(11)]—Means "English, reading and language arts, mathematics, science, foreign languages, civics and government, economics, arts, history, and geography."
Statutory Sec. 602(5). "Elementary School." Nonprofit institutional day or residential school providing elementary education, as determined by State law.	*Sec. 300.13. "Elementary School."* Provision is the same, with the addition of "public elementary charter school."

1999 Regulations (IDEA '97, P.L. 105-17)	2006 Regulations (IDEA '04, P.L. 108-446)
Sec. 300.12. "Evaluation." Procedures to determine whether a child has a disability and the nature and extent of special education and related services needed.	*Sec. 300.15. "Evaluation."* Provision has not changed.
Sec. 300.13. "Free Appropriate Public Education." (FAPE) Special education and related services that (a) are provided at public expense, under public supervision and direction, and without charge; (b) meet SEA standards; (c) include preschool, elementary, or secondary school education; and, (d) are provided through an individualized education program (IEP).	*Sec. 300.17. "Free Appropriate Public Education."* Provision remains the same, with the addition of "*appropriate* preschool, elementary school, or secondary school education. . . .""

"Highly Qualified." No comparable language.	*Sec. 300.18. "Highly Qualified Special Education Teachers." (HQT)*
	
	1. Who is Covered:
	  a. HQT applies to special education teachers teaching core academic subjects in public elementary or secondary schools.
	  b. Public elementary or secondary teachers who are not teaching core academic subjects are "highly qualified" if they meet the general requirements for all special education teachers (#2 below) or alternative route requirements (#3 below).
	  c. HQT does not apply to private school teachers, including those hired or contracted by an LEA to teach parentally placed private school children with disabilities.

d. Fully certified general education teachers who earn full special education certification or licensure are considered new special education teachers for purposes of HQT.

e. Teachers deemed highly qualified under this provision are considered highly qualified for purposes of NCLB.

2. Requirements for All Special Education Teachers:

a. All special education teachers come under the NCLB definition [Sec. 9101(23)]; *PLUS, special education teachers must:*

b. Have State special education certification or have passed State licensing exam, and have license to teach special education;

c. Have not had certification or licensure waived on emergency, temporary, or provisional basis; and,

d. Have at least a bachelor's degree.

3. Alternative Routes to Certification:

Teachers are considered to meet the requirements for "all special education teachers" (#2 above) if they are participating in an alternative route to special education certification under which

a. They receive pre-service and ongoing high-quality professional development, have intensive supervision, teach for not more than three years under the alternative certification,

7

demonstrate satisfactory progress toward full certification; and,

b. The State ensures, through its licensure or certification process, that teachers meet these requirements.

4. Special Education Teachers Teaching Children under Alternate Achievement Standards: Used for teachers teaching core academic subjects *only* to children assessed against alternate standards, as established under NCLB regulations.
   a. Must either meet NCLB Highly Qualified requirements for any new or veteran teacher; or,
   b. Meet NCLB requirements for elementary teachers or middle or high school teachers with subject knowledge appropriate to the level of instruction being provided.

5. Special Education Teachers Teaching Multiple Subjects: Applicable to those teaching 2 or more core academic subjects *only* to children with disabilities.
   a. Must either meet NCLB highly qualified requirements for any new or veteran teacher; or,
   b. If not a new teacher, must demonstrate competence in all subjects taught, as under NCLB, which may include a "high objective uniform State standard of evaluation" (HOUSSE) covering multiple subjects; or,

    c. If a new teacher, who is highly qualified in math, language arts, or science, must demonstrate competence in other core subjects taught, as under NCLB, which may include a HOUSSE, *not later than 2 years after being hired.*

6. Special Education HOUSSE: States may develop a separate HOUSSE for special education teachers,
    a. Provided it does not establish a lower standard for content knowledge than the regular education HOUSSE; and,
    b. Which may be a single HOUSSE evaluation covering multiple subjects.

7. This definition does not create a right of action by a single student or class of students for failure of the teacher to be highly qualified. However, parents may file State complaints regarding staff qualifications.

"Highly Qualified." The addition of this definition to the IDEA is very significant. The NCLB definition of "highly qualified" refers to "any public elementary or secondary school teacher." Considerable debate ensued after the passage of NCLB regarding whether special education teachers, who are not specifically mentioned in NCLB, would also be required to meet the highly qualified provisions of that law. The debate was particularly intense because NCLB requires that new teachers teaching multiple core subjects, as defined in NCLB and now in the IDEA, have an academic major or advanced degree or pass a competency exam in each subject area taught. Veteran teachers under NCLB may demonstrate competency based on a "high objective uniform State standard of evaluation" (HOUSSE), which may involve multiple measures of teacher competency as established by the individual State.

Because middle or high school special education teachers working in a resource capacity provide assistance to students in the full range of academic subject areas, the standard for new teachers would have proven particularly difficult for most special education teachers to meet. Therefore, the IDEA allows special educators teaching multiple core subjects to (a) meet either the NCLB requirements for new or veteran teachers; (b) meet the HOUSSE option; or, (c) for teachers already deemed highly qualified in math, language arts, or science, establish competence in any other core areas taught not later than two years after being hired.

According to the conference report accompanying the IDEA amendments (H. Rep. No. 108-77, Nov. 17, 2004, p. 171), special education teachers providing only consultative services to general education teachers should be considered "highly qualified" if they meet the requirements for "all special education teachers," as outlined above (Sec. 602(10)(A)). Consultative services do not include direct instruction in core academic subjects, but may include adjustments to the learning environment, modification of instructional methods, and curriculum adaptations.

The IDEA regulations also address special education teachers who meet certification or licensure standards through alternative routes. This is particularly significant, since there continues to be a serious shortage of special education personnel. The regulations make clear, however, that individuals deemed "highly qualified" under alternative routes to certification must demonstrate that they are working toward full State certification and may only teach under the alternative certification for a maximum of three years. This provision should assist in filling serious teacher shortages, while also maintaining a quality workforce.

1999 Regulations (IDEA '97, P.L. 105-17)	2006 Regulations (IDEA '04, P.L. 108-446)
"Homeless Children." No comparable language.	*Sec. 300.19. "Homeless Children."* Adds definition from McKinney-Vento Homeless Assistance Act (Sec. 725)— Children who don't have a regular, adequate nighttime residence, including children (a) sharing others' housing due to loss of housing, economic hardship, or similar reason; living in motels, hotels, trailer parks, or campgrounds due to lack of alternative adequate accommodations; living in emergency or transitional shelters; abandoned in hospitals; or

awaiting foster care placement;
(b) whose primary nighttime residence
is a public or private place not
designed for or ordinarily used for
regular sleeping accommodation;
(c) living in cars, public spaces,
abandoned buildings, substandard
housing, bus or train stations, or
similar settings; and, (d) who are
migratory youth living in circumstances
described in (a)–(c).

"Limited English Proficient." No
comparable language.

Sec. 300.27. "Limited English Proficient."
Adds definition from NCLB
[Sec. 9101(25)]: An individual, aged
3–21, enrolled or preparing to enroll in
an elementary or secondary school,

1. (a) who wasn't born in the U.S. or
   whose native language isn't
   English;
   (b) who is a Native American or
   Alaska Native, or native
   resident of the outlying areas
   and comes from an environment where a language other
   than English has significantly
   impacted level of English
   language proficiency; or,
   (c) who is migratory, with native
   language other than English,
   from an environment where a
   language other than English is
   dominant; and,

2. Whose difficulties in speaking,
   reading, writing, or understanding
   English may be sufficient to deny
   the child (a) the ability to meet

proficient level of achievement on State assessments; (b) the ability to successfully achieve in class where instruction is in English; or, (c) the opportunity to participate fully in society.

"Ward of the State." No comparable language.	*Sec. 300.45. "Ward of the State."* Adds new definition—A child who, as determined by State of residence, is a foster child, ward of the State, or in custody of a public child welfare agency. Does not include foster children whose foster parents meet the IDEA "parent" definition.

"Homeless Children," "Limited English Proficient," and "Ward of the State." These additions clarify that every child who is a "child with a disability" under the law must be provided special education and related services and receive the protections of the IDEA, regardless of socioeconomic, language, or other differences. While the spirit and intent of the law has always provided that all children with disabilities needing special education and related services are located and served, the law has never specified these categories of children.

Secs. 300.15; 300.16; 300.17. "Individualized Education Program" (IEP); "IEP Team"; "Individualized Family Service Plan" (IFSP).	*Secs. 300.22; 300.23; 300.24. "IEP"; "IEP Team"; "IFSP."* Provisions have not changed.

a. IEP: written plan of special education and related services for each child.
b. IEP team: Group designated to develop, review, and revise the IEP.
c. IFSP: Written plan for infants and toddlers with disabilities.

1999 Regulations (IDEA '97, P.L. 105-17)	2006 Regulations (IDEA '04, P.L. 108-446)
Part C, Sec. 303.16. "Infants and Toddlers with Disabilities." Defines children with disabilities under age 3 who are eligible for services under IDEA-Part C ("Infants and Toddlers with Disabilities").	*Sec. 300.25. "Infant or Toddler with a Disability."* The definition remains the same as in the previous law. However, it was previously found in 34 CFR Part 303 (regulations on IDEA-Part C). The definition has been included in this part of the law, so that school personnel and families do not have to refer to another document for the definition of eligible children.
Sec. 300.19. "Native Language." 1. In reference to an individual of limited English proficiency, the term means: (a) the language normally used by that individual, or, in the case of a child, the language normally used by the child's parents; (b) in all direct contact with the child (including evaluation), the child's normal language in the home or learning environment. 2. For individuals with deafness or blindness, or individuals with no written language, the term means the individual's normal mode of communication (e.g., sign language, Braille, or oral communication).	*Sec. 300.29. "Native Language."* Provision has not changed.
Sec. 300.20. "Parent." 1. "Parent" means (a) natural or adoptive parents; (b) guardians, but not the State if the child is a ward of the State; (c) persons acting in place of a parent (such as grandparents or stepparents with the child or a person who is legally responsible for the	*Sec. 300.30. "Parent."* Provision is basically the same, with the following changes: 1. "Parent" means: (a) "biological or adoptive parent" (**Note:** Statute uses "natural," rather than "biological"; however, intent and

13

child's welfare); or, surrogate parents.

2. Unless prohibited by State law, States may allow foster parents to act as a parent for purposes of the IDEA, if (a) the natural parents' authority to make educational decisions has been terminated; and, (b) the foster parent has an ongoing, long-term relationship with the child, is willing to make educational decisions, and has no conflict of interest.

meaning are the same.); (b) "foster parent, unless State law, regulations, or contractual obligations with a State or local entity prohibit. . . .";
(c) guardians generally authorized to act as the child's parent or authorized to make educational decisions (but not the State if the child is a ward of the State);
(d) individuals acting in place of biological or adoptive parents (including grandparents, stepparents, or other relatives) with whom the child lives, or an individual legally responsible for the child's welfare; or (e) surrogate parents.

2. When more than one party is qualified to act as a parent, the biological or adoptive parents are presumed to be parents for purposes of educational decision-making, unless they lack legal authority to do so.

3. An individual designated as "parent" by a judicial decree will be the parent for educational decision-making purposes under the IDEA.

Sec. 300.23. "Qualified Personnel." Personnel who have met SEA-approved or recognized certification, licensing, registration, or other comparable requirements applied to the area in which services are provided.

"Qualified Personnel." This provision was deleted in 2004. The basic language is found now in Sec. 300.156, "Personnel Qualifications," and refers generally to related services personnel.

1999 Regulations (IDEA '97, P.L. 105-17)	2006 Regulations (IDEA '04, P.L. 108-446)

Sec. 300.24. "Related Services." Transportation and developmental, corrective, and supportive services, as required to assist the child to benefit from special education, including speech-language pathology and audiology services, psychological services, physical and occupational therapy, recreation, including therapeutic recreation, early identification and assessment of disabilities, counseling, including rehabilitation counseling, orientation and mobility services, medical services for diagnostic or evaluation purposes, school health services, social work services in schools, and parent counseling and training.
 	
Each of these services is defined in the regulations.
	Sec. 300.34. "Related Services." One change to a current service (Orientation and Mobility) was made, and several new provisions were added, as follows:
	
	1. "Orientation and Mobility Services": Added "teaching blind or visually impaired children to use service animals, as appropriate."
	
	New provisions:
	
	1. Adds "Exception for Services Related to Surgically Implanted Devices":
	  a. Surgically implanted medical devices, including the optimization of their functioning or maintenance, are not "related services."
	  b. Receipt of related services by children with such devices is determined by the IEP team, and having such a device cannot limit receipt of those services.
	  c. LEAs must monitor and maintain medical devices that are needed to maintain the child's health and safety, while the child is being transported to and from and is at school.
	  d. LEAs may perform routine checks of external components of surgically implanted devices to assure proper functioning.
	
	2. Adds new related services:
	  a. "Interpreting services": For children who are deaf or hard of hearing, "interpreting services"

means oral transliteration services, cued language transliteration services, sign language transliteration and interpreting services, and transcription services, such as communication access real-time translation (CART), C-Print, and TypeWell; and special interpreting services for children who are deaf-blind.

4. "School Nurse Services": Distinguishes that school nurse services must be provided by a "qualified school nurse," while school health services may be provided by a school nurse or "other qualified person."

"Related Services." The Department has consistently interpreted the list of related services as non-exhaustive, and the discussion to the 2006 regulations continues this interpretation. Services that are not specifically listed must be provided, if determined necessary by the IEP team, for the child to benefit from special education.

The most significant change in this section is the addition of an exception for surgically implanted devices. "Related services" are those services that are necessary for a child to benefit from special education services. Medical services that are required for general daily functioning are not considered related services. This section clarifies that mapping or optimization, i.e., adjusting the electrical stimulation levels of cochlear implants, or the costs of doing so, is not the responsibility of the school district. These services ensure the implant is working properly and must be provided by medical professionals. School personnel can be expected to ensure that the external parts of the device are operating properly, e.g., whether the batteries are charged, volume settings are correct, and cables are properly connected, so that the child can participate fully in special education services.

1999 Regulations (IDEA '97, P.L. 105-17)	2006 Regulations (IDEA '04, P.L. 108-446)
"Scientifically Based Research." No comparable language.	*Sec. 300.35. "Scientifically Based Research."* Adds NCLB definition [Sec. 9101(37)]—Research that applies rigorous, systematic, objective procedures to obtain reliable and valid knowledge, including evaluation using experimental or quasi-experimental designs.
Sec. 300.25. Secondary School. Nonprofit institutional day or residential school providing secondary education, as determined by State law, not including education beyond grade 12.	*Sec. 300.36. Secondary School.* Definition is the same, with the addition of "public secondary charter school that provides secondary education."
"Services Plan." No comparable language.	*Sec. 300.37. "Services Plan."* A written statement describing the special education and related services that an LEA will provide to parentally placed private school children with disabilities, including the location of the services and any transportation necessary, developed and implemented consistent with Secs. 300.137–300.139.
"Secretary." No comparable language.	*Sec. 300.38. "Secretary."* The U.S. Secretary of Education.
Sec. 300.26. "Special Education." 1. Specially designed instruction, at no cost to parents, to meet the child's unique needs, including instruction conducted in the classroom, home, hospitals and institutions, and in other settings, and instruction in physical education (including adapted physical education).	*Sec. 300.39. "Special Education."* Provision has not changed.

2. Includes each of the following if
   they meet the requirements of #1:
   (a) speech-language pathology, or
   any other related service considered
   special education rather than a
   related service under State law;
   (b) travel training; and (c) vocational
   education.

3. "Specially designed instruction"
   means adapting, as appropriate to
   the child's needs, the content,
   methodology, or delivery of
   instruction to (a) meet the child's
   unique needs resulting from the
   disability; and (b) to ensure access
   to the general curriculum, so that
   the child can meet the educational
   standards that apply to all children
   in that jurisdiction.

Sec. 300.28. "Supplementary Aids and Services." Aids, services, and other supports to enable children with disabilities to be educated, to the maximum extent appropriate, in regular education classes and other education-related settings.	*Sec. 300.42. "Supplementary Aids and Services."* Adds aids, services, and other supports provided in "extracurricular and nonacademic settings."

Sec. 300.29. "Transition Services." 1. Coordinated set of activities (a) designed to promote movement from school to post-school activities, including postsecondary education, vocational training, integrated employment, continuing and adult education, independent living or community participation; (b) is based	*Sec. 300.43. "Transition Services."* Additions include: 1. Services must be focused on improving academic and functional achievement. 2. The child's "strengths" must also be taken into account.

on students' needs and taking into account preferences and interests; and, (c) includes instruction, related services, community experiences, employment and post-school objectives, and, if appropriate, acquisition of daily living skills and functional vocational evaluations.	
2. Transition services may be special education if provided as specially designed instruction, or related services if necessary for the child to benefit from special education.	
"Universal Design." No comparable language.	*Sec. 300.44. "Universal Design."* Adds definition from the Assistive Technology Act of 1998 (Sec. 3)— "A concept or philosophy for designing and delivering products and services that are usable by people with the widest possible range of functional capabilities, which include products and services that are directly usable (without requiring assistive technologies) and products and services that are made usable with assistive technologies."

"Universal Design." With few exceptions, children with disabilities are expected to meet the same high academic standards as nondisabled children using the general education curriculum. The dearth of instructional materials and assessment tools that are accessible, valid, and appropriate for use with children with the broad range of disabilities has made this goal more difficult. The concept of universal design is incorporated throughout the amendments to the law. The law allows States to use federal funds to support technology with universal design principles, requires that States and school districts develop and

19

administer assessments, to the extent feasible, using these principles; and, directs research toward incorporating universal design into the development of standards, assessments, curricula, and instructional methods.

PART B—State Eligibility

1999 Regulations (IDEA '97, P.L. 105-17)	2006 Regulations (IDEA '04, P.L. 108-446)
FAPE Requirements	**FAPE Requirements**
Sec. 300.121. Free Appropriate Public Education (FAPE).	*Sec. 300.101(c). Free Appropriate Public Education.*
1. (a) States must ensure that all eligible children with disabilities, ages 3 through 21, including children suspended or expelled from school, have the right to FAPE; and, (b) FAPE must be available children beginning no later than the third birthday; an IEP or IFSP must be in effect by that date; and, if the child's third birthday is in the summer, the IEP team decides when services will begin.	1. Regulations related to FAPE for children removed for disciplinary reasons have been moved to the Discipline provisions (Secs. 300.530–300.536).
2. LEAs do not have to provide services for disciplinary removals, if the child has been removed for 10 school days or less in the school year, if services are not provided for nondisabled children. a. If the child is removed for more than 10 school days in the school year, services must be provided, (1) As necessary to enable the child to progress in the general curriculum and advance toward meeting IEP goals, provided (a) the child	2. The remainder of the provision is the same with the following addition: FAPE must be available to eligible children with disabilities, *despite their not having failed or been retained in a course or grade.*

is removed by school personnel under the discipline provisions and removal does not constitute a change in placement; or, (b) for behavior that is not a manifestation of the child's disability; and

(2) In an interim alternative educational setting, if the removal was for drug or weapons offenses, or maintaining the current placement was substantially likely to result in injury to the child or others.

b. School personnel, in consultation, with the child's special education teacher, determines services for short-term removals; and, the IEP team determines services if the behavior was not a manifestation of the disability.

3. FAPE must be available to children with disabilities who need special education and related services, even though they are advancing from grade to grade.

Free Appropriate Public Education. Provision of special education and related services must support children with disabilities to progress in the general education curriculum. Children who do not fail or are not retained and who progress from grade to grade continue to be eligible for special education and related services, unless the IEP team makes an individual determination that those services and supports are no longer necessary.

Sec. 300.122. Exception to FAPE for Certain Ages.

1. The obligation to make FAPE available does not apply to:
   a. Children ages 3, 4, 5, 18, 19, 20, or 21 in States where providing FAPE to those children would be inconsistent with State law or practice or court order regarding provision of public education to children in one or more of those age groups.
   b. Students ages 18–21 to the extent State law does not require special education services be provided to students, who, in their last educational placement prior to incarceration in an adult facility, were not identified as a child with a disability or did not have an IEP.
   c. Children who have graduated from high school with a regular diploma, and graduation with a regular diploma is a change in placement.

2. The exception in 1.b. does *not* apply to students ages 18–21 who (a) had been identified and received services under an IEP, but who left school prior to their incarceration; or, (b) did not have an IEP in their last educational setting, but had been identified as a "child with a disability."

3. ***Preschoolers under Part C.*** No comparable language.

Sec. 300.102. Exceptions to FAPE for Certain Ages. Additions include:

1. "Regular high school diploma" does not include an "alternative degree" that is not fully aligned with State academic standards, e.g., a certificate or a general educational development credential (GED).

2. The FAPE requirement does not apply to children, ages 3–5, eligible for preschool services, but whose parents opt for their children to remain in early intervention services (Part C "Infants and Toddlers" program).

Other FAPE Requirements	Other FAPE Requirements
Sec. 300.301. FAPE—Methods and Payments. 1. States may use whatever State, local, federal, and private resources are available to meet the requirements of the law, e.g., States may use interagency cost-sharing agreements to pay for costs such as residential placement. 2. Insurers or other third party payors are not relieved from valid obligations to provide or pay for services. 3. States must ensure that implementation of IEPs is not delayed, including where the payment source is being determined.	*Sec. 300.103. FAPE—Methods and Payments.* Provision has not changed.
Sec. 300.302. Residential Placement. If placement in a public or private residential program is necessary to provide a child with special education and related services, the program including non-medical care and room and board must be at no cost to the parents.	*Sec. 300.104. Residential Placement.* Provision has not changed.
Sec. 300.308. Assistive Technology. 1. A child must be given assistive technology devices or services, or both, if required as part of special education, related services, or supplementary aids and services.	*Sec. 300.105. Assistive Technology.* Provision has not changed.

2. On a case-by-case basis, children may use school-purchased assistive technology devices at home or in other settings, if the IEP team determines the child needs access to those devices to receive FAPE.	

Sec. 300.309. Extended School Year Services. (ESY)	**Sec. 300.106. Extended School Year Services.** Provision has not changed.
1. ESY must be available if the IEP team determines, on an individual basis, that extended year services are necessary to provide FAPE.	
2. LEAs may not (a) limit ESY to particular disability categories; or, (b) unilaterally limit type, amount, or duration of ESY.	
3. "ESY" means special education and related services that (a) are provided beyond the normal school year, in accordance with the IEP, and at no cost to parents; and, (b) meet SEA standards.	

Sec. 300.306. Nonacademic Services.	**Sec. 300.107. Nonacademic Services.** Provision remains the same, with the following addition:
1. LEAs must take steps to provide nonacademic and extracurricular services and activities in a way that affords children with disabilities an equal opportunity to participate.	LEAs "must take steps, *including the provision of supplementary aid and services determined appropriate and necessary by the child's IEP team*, to provide nonacademic and extracurricular services and activities. . . ."
2. Those services and activities may include counseling services, athletics, transportation, health services, recreational activities, school-sponsored special interests	

groups, referrals to agencies that provide assistance to individuals with disabilities, and employment.

Sec. 300.307. Physical Education.

1. P.E. services, specially designed if necessary, must be made available to every child receiving FAPE, and children must be afforded the opportunity to participate in P.E. unless (a) enrolled full time in a separate facility; or, (b) they need specially designed P.E., as prescribed in the IEP.

2. If the child needs specially designed P.E., the LEA must provide services directly or arrange for provision of services.

3. For children in separate facilities, the LEA must ensure P.E. services are provided.

Sec. 300.108. Physical Education.
Provision remains the same, with the following addition:

P.E. must be made available to children with disabilities, unless P.E. is not provided to nondisabled children in the same grades.

Secs. 300.123; 300.124. Full Educational Opportunity Goal (FEOG).
The SEA must have policies and procedures that establish a goal of providing full educational opportunity to all children with disabilities, ages birth through 21, and a timetable for accomplishing that goal.

Sec. 300.109. Full Educational Opportunity (FEOG). Provision has not changed.

Sec. 300.305. Program Options. LEAs
must take steps to make available the variety of educational programs and services that are available to nondisabled children served by the

Sec. 300.110. Program Options.
Provision has not changed.

LEA, including art, music,
industrial arts, consumer and
homemaking education, and
vocational education.

***Secs. 300.125; 300.313. Child Find;
Children Experiencing Developmental
Delay.***

1. States must ensure that all children
with disabilities living in the State,
including children in private schools,
regardless of the severity of their
disability, and who need special
education and related services, are
identified, located, and evaluated,
and a method is developed to
determine which children are
currently receiving services.

2. The requirement applies to highly
mobile children, e.g., migrant and
homeless, and children suspected of
being children with disabilities,
despite advancing from grade to
grade.

3. In States where the lead agency for
Part C (Infants and Toddlers) is not
the SEA and the lead agency will
participate in child find, the State
must indicate how this will be
accomplished.

4. The law does not require that
children be classified by their
disability, as long as each eligible
child is regarded as a "child with a
disability" and receives appropriate
services.

Sec. 300.111. Child Find. Provision
remains the same, with the following
addition:

"Homeless children" and "wards of the
State" who may be children with
disabilities in need of special
education and related services must
also be identified, located, and
evaluated.

26

5. Developmental delay:
   a. States that use this term must determine whether it applies to children ages 3 through 9, or a subset of that age range, e.g., 3 through 5.
   b. States may not require LEAs to adopt the term, but, if an LEA uses the term, it must use the State definition and age range; however, if a State does not adopt the term, LEAs in that State may not use the term.
   c. States or LEAs that use the term may also use one or more of the disability categories for any child in the age range, if the child is evaluated, meets the disability definition, and needs special education and related services; and, services must be provided.
   d. States may adopt a common definition of "developmental delay" for use in Parts B and C.

Sec. 300.303. Proper Functioning of Hearing Aids. The LEA must ensure that hearing aids worn by children in school are functioning properly.

Sec. 300.113. Routine Checking of Hearing Aids and External Components of Surgically Implanted Medical Devices. Provision is the same, with the following addition:

LEAs must ensure that external components of surgically implanted devices are working properly, but are not responsible for "post-surgical maintenance, programming, or replacement" of these devices.

1999 Regulations (IDEA '97, P.L. 105-17)	2006 Regulations (IDEA '04, P.L. 108-446)
Least Restrictive Environment (LRE)	Least Restrictive Environment (LRE)

Secs. 300.550; 300.130. LRE Requirements. 1. Except as applied to students with disabilities incarcerated in adult prisons, LEAs must ensure that (a) to the maximum extent appropriate, children with disabilities, including those in public or private institutions or other care facilities, are educated with nondisabled children; and, (b) special classes, separate schooling or other removal from the regular educational environment occurs only if the nature or severity of the disability is such that education in regular classes with supplementary aids and services cannot be satisfactorily achieved. 2. Funding mechanisms where the State distributes its funds on the basis of the type of setting where a child is served may not result in placements that violate LRE (#1 above). 3. If the State does not have policies to ensure compliance with #2, it must provide to the Secretary an assurance that it will revise the mechanism as soon as possible to ensure compliance with LRE.	*Sec. 300.114. LRE Requirements.* Provision remains the same, with the following addition: States must not use funding mechanisms based on types of setting that result in "failure to provide a child with a disability FAPE according to the unique needs of the child, as described in the child's IEP."

1999 Regulations (IDEA '97, P.L. 105-17)	2006 Regulations (IDEA '04, P.L. 108-446)
Sec. 300.551. Continuum of Placements. LEAs must (a) ensure that a continuum of alternative placements, which must include the placements listed in Sec. 300.26 ("Special Education"), is available to meet children's needs for special education and related services; and, (b) provide supplementary services, e.g., resource room or itinerant instruction, in conjunction with regular class placement.	**Sec. 300.115. Continuum of Placements.** Provision has not changed.
Sec. 300.552. Placements. 1. In determining educational placements, including for preschool children, LEAs must ensure that placement decisions are made by a group that includes (a) parents and (b) other persons who are knowledgeable about the child, the meaning of evaluation data, and placement options. 2. Placements must be (a) in compliance with LRE require-ments; determined at least annually, based on the IEP; and, (c) as close as possible to the child's home. 3. Unless the IEP requires otherwise, children attend the school they would attend if they were not disabled. 4. Consideration is given in selecting LRE to any potential harmful effects on the child or quality of services.	**Sec. 300.116. Placements.** Provision has not changed.

1999 Regulations	2006 Regulations
5. Children are not removed from age-appropriate regular classrooms solely because of needed modifications in the general curriculum.	
Sec. 300.553. Nonacademic Settings. LEAs must ensure that children with disabilities participate with nondisabled children, to the maximum extent appropriate, in nonacademic and extracurricular services and activities, e.g., recess periods, meals, and other nonacademic services (See Sec. 300.306).	*Sec. 300.117. Nonacademic Settings.* Provision remains the same with the following addition: LEAS must provide supplementary aids and services, as determined by the IEP team, which are necessary for children to participate in nonacademic and extracurricular activities.
Sec. 300.554. Children in Public or Private Institutions. With the exception of responsibility for some individuals in adult prisons, SEAs must ensure LRE is effectively implemented, including, if necessary making arrangements with the institutions, such as memoranda of agreement or special implementation procedures.	*Sec. 300.118. Children in Public or Private Institutions.* Provision has not changed.
Sec. 300.555. Technical Assistance and Training Activities. SEAs must ensure that teachers and administrators are fully informed about responsibilities for implementing LRE and provided with the necessary technical assistance and training to do so.	*Sec. 300.119. Technical Assistance and Training Activities.* Provision has not changed.

1999 Regulations (IDEA '97, P.L. 105-17)	2006 Regulations (IDEA '04, P.L. 108-446)
Sec. 300.556. Monitoring Activities. SEAs must ensure that LEAs implement LRE. If there is evidence that placements are inconsistent with LRE, the SEA must review the LEA's justification for its action and assist in planning and implementing any necessary corrective action.	**Sec. 300.120. Monitoring Activities.** Provision has not changed.

Additional Eligibility Requirements	Additional Eligibility Requirements
Secs. 300.129; 300.126; 300.127. Procedural Safeguards; Procedures for Evaluation and Determination of Eligibility; Confidentiality of Personally Identifiable Information. Each of these sections simply state that SEAs must ensure that these procedures are met. Details of each procedure are covered in other sections of the law.	**Secs. 300.121; 300.122; 300.123. Procedural Safeguards; Evaluation; Confidentiality of Personally Identifiable Information.** Provisions have not changed.

Sec. 300.132. Transition of Children from Part C to Preschool Programs. 1. SEAs must ensure that children who are in early intervention programs (Part C) and who will participate in preschool programs have a smooth and effective transition from one to the other 2. By the child's third birthday, an IEP or IFSP (if consistent with Sec. 300.342) must be developed and implemented. 3. LEAs must participate in Part C transition planning meetings.	**Sec. 300.124. Transition of Children from Part C to Preschool Programs.** Provision has not changed.

31

1999 Regulations (IDEA '97, P.L. 105-17)	2006 Regulations (IDEA '04, P.L. 108-446)
Children with Disabilities Enrolled by Parents in Private Schools (**Note:** "PSCD" is used by the author in these sections to refer to private school children with disabilities enrolled by their parents.)	*Children with Disabilities Enrolled by Parents in Private Schools* (**Note:** "PSCD" is used by the author in these sections to refer to private school children with disabilities enrolled by their parents.)
Sec. 300.450. Definition of "Private School Children with Disabilities." Means children with disabilities enrolled by their parents in private schools or facilities other than children placed in private schools or facilities by public agencies.	*Sec. 300.130. Definition of Parentally Placed Private School Children with Disabilities.* Provision remains the same with the following addition: "Private schools or facilities" include "religious schools or facilities" that meet the definitions of elementary or secondary schools.
Secs. 300.451; 300.453(c). Child Find for Private School Children with Disabilities; Expenditures. 1. LEAs must locate, identify, and evaluate all private, including religious, school children with disabilities residing in the LEA's jurisdiction. 2. These child find activities must be comparable to child find for public school children. 3. Expenditures for child find activities may not be considered in determining if the LEA has met the formula requirements for expenditures on PSCD.	*Sec. 300.131. Child Find for Parentally Placed Private School Children with Disabilities.* New regulations add the following: 1. General: LEAs must locate, identify, and evaluate all children with disabilities in private, including religious, elementary and secondary schools *located in the school district served by the LEA;* and, the process must be completed in a comparable time period to child find for public school children. 2. Child Find Design: The process must ensure equitable participation of and an accurate count of PSCD. 3. Cost: The cost of individual evaluations may not be considered in meeting the expenditure requirements.

	4. Out-of-State Children: LEAs where private, including religious, schools are located must, for purposes of child find, include PSCD who reside in States other than the State where the private schools they attend are located.
Sec. 300.452. Provision of Services— Basic Requirement. To the extent consistent with their number and location in the State, (a) provision must be made for participation of PSCD in special education and related services; and, (b) services plans must be developed and implemented for each child designated to receive services.	*Sec. 300.132. Provision of Services for Parentally Placed Private School Children with Disabilities—Basic Requirement.* The general requirements remains the same, with the following additions: 1. Provision for participation must be consistent with the number and location of PSCD enrolled in private, including religious, elementary and secondary schools located in the school district served by the LEA. 2. Children may be provided special education and related services, including *direct services* (See Sec. 300.137). 3. Services plans are developed for children designated to receive services *by the LEA in which the private school is located.* 4. LEAs must maintain, and provide to the SEA, information on the number of children (a) evaluated, (b) determined to be "children with disabilities," and (c) served.

Sec. 300.453. Expenditures.	*Sec. 300.133. Expenditures.* Provision remains generally the same, with the following additions:

Sec. 300.453. Expenditures.

1. LEAs must spend on provision of special education and related services to PSCD:
   a. For children aged 3–21, an amount equal to the same proportion of the LEA's total Part B subgrant from the SEA as the number of private school children with disabilities aged 3–21 residing in its jurisdiction is to the total number of children with disabilities in its jurisdiction aged 3–21.
   b. For children aged 3–5, a amount equal to the same proportion of the LEA's total preschool subgrant as the number of private school children with disabilities aged 3–5 residing in the jurisdiction is to the total number of children with disabilities aged 3–5.

2. LEAs must (a) consult with private school representatives to decide how to conduct the annual child count; and, (b) ensure the count is conducted annually on December 1 or the last Friday of October.

3. Expenditures on child find activities may not be considered in determining the requirements of #1 above.

4. SEAs and LEAs may provide services in excess of those required in this section, consistent with State law or local policy.

Sec. 300.133. Expenditures. Provision remains generally the same, with the following additions:

1. Clarifies that:
   a. Services provided may be *direct services.*
   b. Children referred to are only those enrolled by their parents in private, including religious, elementary and secondary schools located in the school district served by the LEA.

2. Children aged 3–5 are considered to be PSCD if the private school they attend meets the "elementary school" definition.

3. If an LEA has not spent all of the federal funds required under the formula by the end of the fiscal year for which those funds were appropriated, the remaining funds must be obligated for special education and related services for PSCD during a one-year carryover period.

4. Calculating the proportionate share: After "timely and meaningful consultation" with private school representatives, LEAs must, through a child find process, determine the number of PSCD in private schools located in the LEA. (**Note:** Appendix B of the regulations contains an example of how "proportionate share" is calculated.)

34

3. Annual child count: After "timely and meaningful consultation" with private school representatives, the LEA annually must determine the number of PSCD in its jurisdiction through a child count conducted on any date between October 1 and December 1; and, the count is used to determine the amount that LEAs must spend on services for PSCD.

4. State and local funds may supplement, but not supplant, the proportionate amount of federal funds that must be spent on this population.

Sec 300.454. Services Determined.

1. LEAs must have "timely and meaningful" consultation with private school representatives to decide which children will receive services, what services will be provided, how and where those services will be provided, and how services will be evaluated.

2. Private school representatives must have a genuine opportunity to express their views on each of the matters in #1 above.

3. Consultation must occur before LEAs make decisions affecting the opportunity of PSCD to participate in services.

Sec. 300.134. Consultation. Additions and changes include: To ensure timely and meaningful consultation, LEAs, or if appropriate, SEAs, must consult with private school representatives and representatives of PSCD during the development and design of services, regarding:

1. The child find process, including (1) how parents of PSCD suspected of having disabilities may equitably participate; and, (2) how parents, teachers, and private school officials will be informed of the process.

2. Determination of the proportionate share of federal funds available to serve PSCD, including how the share was calculated.

3. The consultation process, including how the process will operate through the school year to ensure continued meaningful participation in services.

4. How, where, and by whom services will be provided, including types of services (including direct services and alternate service delivery mechanism), how services will be apportioned if funds are insufficient to serve all PSCD, and how and when those decisions will be made.

5. How, if the LEA disagrees with private school officials on provision or types of services (direct or by contract), the LEA will provide a written explanation of why it chose not to provide services directly or through a contract.

Written Affirmation. No comparable language.

Sec. 300.135. Written Affirmation. When timely and meaningful consultation has occurred, the LEA must obtain a written affirmation signed by the private school representative. If the representative does provide affirmation in a reasonable period of time, the LEA must forward documentation of the process to the SEA.

Sec. 300.457. Complaints. State complaint procedures may be used for complaints that SEAs or LEAs failed to meet requirements of the PSCD provisions.

Sec. 300.136. Compliance. Additions include:

1. Private school officials have the right to file State complaints that LEAs did not (a) engage in

meaningful and timely consultation; or (b) give due consideration to the views of private school officials.

2. Officials must provide the SEA the basis of the LEA's noncompliance with the applicable provisions of the law, and the LEA must forward appropriate documentation to the SEA.

3. If officials are dissatisfied with the SEA's decision, they may submit a complaint to the Secretary, and the SEA must provide appropriate documentation to the Secretary.

Sec. 300.454. Services Determined.

1. No PSCD has an individual right to some or all special education and related services they would receive if enrolled in public school.

2. LEAs must make final decisions regarding provision of services to PSCD.

3. If PSCD in a private or religious school will receive services, the LEA must (a) have meetings to develop, review, and revise a services plan; and, (b) ensure that a private school representative attends each meeting, and, if the representative cannot attend, use other methods to ensure participation, including individual or conference telephone calls.

Sec. 300.137. Equitable Services Determined. Provision has not changed.

Sec. 300.455. Services Provided.

1. Services must be provided by personnel meeting the same standards as personnel providing services in the public schools.

2. PSCD (a) may receive a different amount of services than public school children with disabilities; and, (b) are not entitled to any service or amount of service the child would receive if enrolled in public school.

3. Each PSCD receiving services must have a services plan that describes the specific special education and related services to be provided.

4. Services plans must, to the extent appropriate, meet the requirements and be developed, reviewed, and revised consistent with the law's IEP provisions.

Sec. 300.138. Equitable Services Provided. Provisions are basically the same, with the following additions:

1. Personnel providing services must meet the same standards as personnel providing services in public schools, except that private school teachers do not have to meet the highly qualified special education requirements.

2. Services plans must meet the requirements, to the extent appropriate, of the IEP "content" provisions (Sec. 300.320) or, for children aged 3–5, the Individualized Family Service Plan (IFSP) provisions [Sec. 200.323(b)].

3. Equitable services must be provided by LEA employees or through LEA contract with an individual, association, agency, organization, or other entity.

4. Services, including materials and equipment, must be secular, neutral, and non-ideological.

Sec. 300.456. Location of Services; Transportation.

1. Services to PSCD may be provided on-site at private, including religious, schools, to the extent consistent with law.

2. PSCD must be provided transportation, if necessary for the child to benefit from or participate

Sec. 300. 139. Location of Services; Transportation. Provision has not changed.

in services, (a) from the child's school or home to a site other than the private school; and, (b) from the service site to the private school or child's home, depending on timing of services.	
3. LEAs do not have to provide transportation from the child's home to the private school.	
4. Cost of transportation may be included in whether the LEA has met the expenditure requirements (Sec. 300.453).	
Sec. 300.457. Complaints. Due process procedures do not apply to complaints regarding parentally placed private school children with disabilities, except for complaints regarding child find.	*Sec. 300.140. Due Process Complaints and State Complaints.* 1. Due process complaints on child find requirements must be filed *with the LEA in which the private school is located,* with a copy forwarded to the SEA. 2. Complaints filed by private school officials must be filed with the SEA in accordance with outlined procedures [Sec. 300.136(b)].
Sec. 300.459. Requirement that funds Not Benefit a Private School. LEAs may not use funds (Part B or Preschool) to finance existing levels of instruction in private schools or otherwise benefit those schools. Federal funds must be used to provide services to PSCD, but not for the needs of private schools or the general needs of students enrolled in private schools.	*Sec. 300.141. Requirement that funds Not Benefit a Private School.* Provision has not changed.

1999 Regulations (IDEA '97, P.L. 105-17)	2006 Regulations (IDEA '04, P.L. 108-446)
Secs. 300.460; 300.461. Use of Public School Personnel; Use of Private School Personnel.	**Sec. 300.142. Use of Personnel.** Provisions have not changed.
1. LEAs may use federal funds to make public school personnel available in non-public facilities (a) to the extent necessary to provide services to PSCD; and, (b) if those services are not normally provided by the private school.	
2. LEAs may use federal funds to pay for the services of private school employees to provide services, if private school employees work (a) outside their regular hours; and, (b) under public supervision and control.	
Sec. 300.458. Separate Classes Prohibited. LEAs may not use federal funds for classes that are organized separately on the basis of school enrollment or students' religion if (a) classes are at the same site; and, (b) classes include both public school and private school children.	**Sec. 300.143. Separate Classes Prohibited.** Provision has not changed.

Children with Disabilities Enrolled by Their Parents in Private Schools.

A major change in this section may have a significant impact on LEAs in jurisdictions that are home to multiple private schools or facilities. Previously, the law placed responsibility for child find and provision of services to parentally placed private school children with disabilities on the LEA where the child was a resident. The 2004 amendments shift those responsibilities to the LEA *where the private school or facility is located.*

Two other new provisions may add to the impact on certain LEAs. LEAs must carry over any unexpended funds under the private school formula for another year, and those funds must be spent on private school students. In addition, for children in private preschools where those schools meet the elementary school definition, children aged 3–5 are also covered by these provisions.

The provision regarding qualifications for teachers in private schools is somewhat unclear. While the provision states that the "highly qualified special education teacher" requirements (Sec. 300.18) do not apply to private school teachers, Sec. 300.138 states that services to parentally placed private school children with disabilities must be provided by "personnel meeting the same standards as personnel providing services in the public schools. . . ." In the regulatory discussion, the U.S. Department of Education reiterates that "highly qualified" provisions do not apply to private school teachers, but the Department has not explained the distinction between "highly qualified" and the requirement that private school teachers meet the same standards as public school teachers.

1999 Regulations (IDEA '97, P.L. 105-17)	2006 Regulations (IDEA '04, P.L. 108-446)
Children with Disabilities in Private Schools Placed or Referred by Public Agencies	**Children with Disabilities in Private Schools Placed or Referred by Public Agencies**
Secs. 300.400–300.402. Applicability of Secs. 300.401–300.402; Responsibility of SEA; Implementation by SEA. 1. These provisions are applicable only to children with disabilities placed in or referred to private schools or facilities by a public agency for provision of special education and related services. 2. SEAs shall ensure these children (a) are provided services with an IEP conforming to the requirements of the law, at no cost to parents; (b) are provide an education that meets applicable State standards; and, (c) have all rights of children with disabilities served by the public agency.	*Secs. 300.145–300.147. Applicability of Secs. 300.146–300.147. Responsibility of SEA; Implementation by SEA.* Provisions have not changed.

41

1999 Regulations (IDEA '97, P.L. 105-17)	2006 Regulations (IDEA '04, P.L. 108-446)

3. In implementing these provisions, SEAs must (a) monitor compliance; (b) disseminate applicable standards to private schools and facilities serving these children; and, (c) provide those private schools and facilities an opportunity to participate in development and revision of applicable State standards.

Children with Disabilities Enrolled by Their Parents in Private Schools When FAPE is at Issue	Children with Disabilities Enrolled by Their Parents in Private Schools When FAPE is at Issue

Sec. 300.403. Placement of Children by Parents if FAPE is at Issue.

1. LEAs are not required to pay for education costs, including special education and related services for children with disabilities at private schools or facilities if the LEA made FAPE available and parents chose to place the child in the private school or facility; and, LEAs must include those children in the group whose needs are addressed in Secs. 300.450–300.462.

2. Disagreements between parents and LEAs regarding availability of appropriate programs and financial responsibility are subject to due process procedures.

3. If parents of a child who previously received services from the LEA enroll the child in a private preschool or elementary or

Sec. 300.148. Placement of Children by Parents if FAPE is at Issue. Provision has remained basically the same, with the following addition:

The cost of reimbursement "may, *in the discretion of the court or a hearing officer,* not be reduced for failure . . ." to inform the LEA of rejection of the public placement.

secondary school without consent of or referral by the LEA, a court or hearing officer may require the LEA to reimburse the parents for costs of enrollment if there is a finding that the LEA did not make FAPE available prior to enrollment in a timely manner and that the private school placement is appropriate.

4. A Parental placement may be found appropriate, even if it does not meet State standards applicable to public education.

5. Cost of reimbursement may be reduced or denied if, (a) (1) at the most recent IEP meeting prior to removal of the child from public school, parents did not inform the IEP team that they were rejecting the public placement, including their concerns and intent to enroll the child in private school; or, (2) at least 10 business days prior to removal, parents did not give written notice of information in (a); (b) if, prior to parents' removal of the child, LEA informed them, through notice provisions, of intent to evaluate the child, but parents did not produce the child; or, (c) upon a judicial finding of unreasonableness regarding the parents' actions.

6. Costs may not be reduced or denied for failure to provide notice if (a) the parent is illiterate and cannot write in English; (b) compliance

with #5(a) above would likely result in physical or serious emotional harm to the child; (c) the school prevented parents from providing notice; or, (d) parents had not received notice of the notice requirement.

SEA Responsibility for General Supervision and Implementation of Procedural Safeguards

Sec. 300.600. Responsibility for All Educational Programs.

1. SEAs are responsible for ensuring that all requirements of the law are carried out, and that each educational program for children with disabilities in the State, including those administered by any other State or local agency, (a) is under the SEA's general supervision; and, (b) meets the SEA's education standards.

2. The IDEA does not limit responsibilities of agencies other than education agencies for providing or paying some or all costs of FAPE to children in the State.

3. Governors, or other individuals pursuant to State law, may assign responsibility to any public agency in the State for ensuring this law is met for children with disabilities incarcerated in adult prisons.

SEA Responsibility for General Supervision and Implementation of Procedural Safeguards

Sec. 300.149. SEA Responsibility for General Supervision.

Provisions remain the same, with the following additions:

1. SEAs are not responsible for education programs in elementary and secondary schools for Indian children operated or funded by the Secretary of the Interior.

2. SEAs must ensure that, in regard to homeless children, applicable requirements of the McKinney-Vento Homeless Assistance Act are met.

3. SEAs must have policies and procedures to comply with the monitoring and enforcement provisions (Secs. 300.660–300.602; 300.606–300.608).

1999 Regulations (IDEA '97, P.L. 105-17)	2006 Regulations (IDEA '04, P.L. 108-446)
Sec. 300.143. SEA Implementation of Procedural Safeguards. The State must have procedures that the SEA (and any agency assigned responsibility under Sec. 300.600) follows to inform public agencies of their responsibilities for implementation of procedural safeguards.	***Sec. 300.150. SEA Implementation of Procedural Safeguards.*** Provision has not changed.
State Complaint Procedures	**State Complaint Procedures**

Sec. 300.660. Adoption of State Complaint Procedures.
 	
1. SEAs must:
  a. Adopt written procedures for resolving complaints, including complaints filed by organizations or individuals from another State that meet requirements of Sec. 300.662 by (1) providing for filing complaints with the SEA, and (2) at the SEA's discretion, providing for filing complaints with LEAs and the right to have SEA review of the LEA decision
  b. Widely disseminate State complaint procedures to parents and other interested parties.
 	
2. In resolving complaints where failure to provide appropriate services has been found, SEAs must address (a) how to remediate the denial of services, including monetary reimbursement, as appropriate, or other corrective actions; and, (b) appropriate future provision of services.
	Sec. 300.151. Adoption of State Complaint Procedures. Provision remains basically the same, with the following addition:
	
	"Compensatory services" may also be a remedy for failure to provide appropriate services.

1999 Regulations (IDEA '97, P.L. 105-17)	2006 Regulations (IDEA '04, P.L. 108-446)

Sec. 300.661. Minimum State Complaint Procedures.

1. SEA complaint procedures must include a 60-day time limit after complaints are filed to (a) carry out an independent investigation, if deemed necessary; (b) give the complainant an opportunity to submit additional information about the allegations in the complaint; (c) review all relevant information and make an independent determination regarding whether a violation has occurred; and, (d) issue a written decision.

2. Time extensions must be allowed only in exceptional circumstances.

3. Procedures for effective implementation of the SEA's final decision must be available, if needed, including technical assistance, negotiations, and corrective actions.

4. If written complaints are received that are also the subject of a due process hearing or contain multiple issues, any of which are part of a hearing, SEAs must set aside those parts of the complaints until the hearing is concluded; however, issues not part of the hearing must be resolved within prescribed timelines.

5. If a complaint contains an issue previously decided in a due process hearing with the same parties, (a) the hearing decision is binding;

Sec. 300.152. Minimum State Complaint Procedures. Provision is basically the same, with the following additions:

1. LEAs have the opportunity to respond to the complaint, including at a minimum, at the LEA's discretion, a proposal to resolve the complaint and an opportunity for the LEA and the parent to voluntarily engage in mediation.

2. A time extension is allowed only in exceptional circumstances, or where the parent and the LEA agree to extend the time to use mediation or other alternative means of dispute resolution if available in the State.

(b) SEAs must inform the complainant; and, (c) complaints alleging an LEA's failure to implement a due process decision must be resolved by the SEA.

Sec. 300.662. Filing a Complaint.

1. Organizations or individuals may file written complaints with the State, which must include a statement that the LEA has violated a requirement of the Act and the facts on which the statement is based.

2. The complaint must allege a violation that occurred not more than one year prior to the date the complaint is received, unless a longer period is reasonable, due to an ongoing violation or a request for compensatory services for a violation that occurred more than three years before the complaint was received.

Sec. 300.153. Filing a Complaint.

Additions to the regulations include:

1. The complaint also must include (a) signature and contact information for the complainant; (b) if alleging violations regarding a specific child, the child's name and address and school, or for a homeless child, available contact information and school; (c) a description of the nature of the problem and any facts related to the problem; and, (d) a proposed resolution to the problem to the extent known at the time the complaint is filed.

2. A copy of the complaint must be sent to the LEA or public agency serving the child at the same time the complaint is filed with the SEA.

Methods of Ensuring Services

Methods of Ensuring Services

Sec. 300.142. Methods of Ensuring Services.
The Governor or designee must ensure that an interagency agreement is in effect between the SEA and non-education public agencies that may be responsible for providing or paying for special education and related services. For children covered by public

Sec. 300.154. Methods of Ensuring Services.
Provision remains the same, with the following addition:

Regarding children covered by public benefits/insurance, the public agency must (a) obtain parental consent each time it seeks to access public benefits/insurance; and, (b) notify

1999 Regulations	2006 Regulations
benefits/insurance, the public agency may use Medicaid or other public benefits/insurance to provide or pay for services.	parents that their refusal to allow access to those benefits does not relieve the agency of its responsibility to ensure that required services are provided at no cost to parents.

Additional State Eligibility Requirements	**Additional State Eligibility Requirements**
Sec. 300.135. Comprehensive System of Personnel Development. The SEA is required to develop a system to ensure an adequate supply of qualified special education, regular education, and related services personnel.	*Comprehensive System of Personnel Development.* This provision was deleted in the 2004 IDEA amendments. The State Personnel Development Grants (Part D, Subpart 1) incorporate most of what was previously required in this section.

Sec. 300.136. Personnel Standards.	*Sec. 300.156. Personnel Qualifications.*
1. SEAs must establish and maintain standards to ensure that personnel are appropriately and adequately prepared and trained. Standards must be consistent with any State-approved or recognized certification or licensure or other comparable requirements. 2. To the extent those standards are not based on the highest State entry requirement applicable to a specific profession or discipline, the State must take steps to retrain or hire personnel that meet the highest requirements. 3. State standards must include provision for appropriately trained and supervised paraprofessionals and assistants to assist in provision of services.	"Standards" has been replaced with "qualifications" in the statute and regulations in provisions regarding personnel. Also, the "highest requirement" language, including the three-year waiver for personnel to meet the highest requirement, has been eliminated. Other changes include: 1. Related services personnel must meet any State-approved or State-recognized certification, licensure, registration, or other comparable requirements. Personnel may not have had licensure or certification waived on an emergency, temporary, or provisional basis. 2. Public school special education teachers must be highly qualified by the deadline established in NCLB [Sec. 1119(a)(2)].

1999 Regulations (IDEA '97, P.L. 105-17)	2006 Regulations (IDEA '04, P.L. 108-446)
4. SEAs may require LEAs to make ongoing good faith efforts to recruit and hire appropriately and adequately trained personnel, including, where there are shortages in a particular discipline, individuals who will meet the highest standard within three years.	3. LEAs are required to take "measurable steps" to recruit, hire, train, and retain highly qualified personnel.
5. States may allow paraprofessionals and assistants who are appropriately trained and supervised, according to State law or policy, to assist in providing special education and related services.	

Personnel Qualifications. While qualifications for special education teachers are governed by the "highly qualified" provisions in the federal statute, qualifications for related services personnel are left to the States. The Conference Committee stated its intention that SEAs establish "rigorous qualifications" for related services personnel and encouraged SEAs to consult with other State agencies, LEAs, and the professional organizations representing service providers in designing these qualifications. The Department declined to regulate consultation, but acknowledged that such consultation would be good practice. The Department also noted in the regulatory discussion that States should have the "flexibility, based on each State's unique circumstances, to determine how best to establish and maintain standards for providers. . . ."

Sec. 300.137. Performance Goals and Indicators. States must establish performance goals consistent with standards for nondisabled students. States must have performance indicators to assess progress toward meeting performance goals that, at a minimum, address performance on assessments and dropout and graduation rates. States will report	*Sec. 300.157. Performance Goals and Indicators.* Additions include:
	1. Performance goals must be the same as the State's objectives for progress by children with disabilities in its definition of adequate yearly progress under NCLB and must address graduations and dropout rates *and*

every two years to the Secretary and the public on the progress of children with disabilities and the State toward meeting the performance goals.	*other factors as the State may determine.*
	2. States must also have measurable annual objectives for progress of children with disabilities under NCLB [Sec. 1111(b)(2) (C)(v)(II)(cc)].
	3. States must report annually on progress toward meeting goals, which may include elements of the reports required under NCLB [Sec. 1111(h)].

Performance Goals and Indicators: Performance goals for students with disabilities must conform to the State's definition of "adequate yearly progress" (AYP) under NCLB. AYP is a measure established by each State to demonstrate students' progress in meeting proficiency on assessments based on the State's academic achievement standards. Students with disabilities constitute a specific subgroup under NCLB, and data on those students' progress must be disaggregated and publicly reported.

Secs. 300.138; 300.139. Participation in Assessments; Reports Relating to Assessments.	*Statutory Sec. 612(a)(16). Participation in Assessments.*
1. Children with disabilities will be included in general State- and district-wide assessments, with appropriate accommodations and modifications in administration.	1. *All* children with disabilities participate in *all* assessments, with accommodations and alternate assessments as indicated on the IEP.
2. As appropriate, the SEA or LEA must develop guidelines for participation in and develop and conduct alternate assessments for children who cannot participate in State- and district-wide assessments.	2. SEA, or for district-wide assessments LEA, guidelines must provide for alternate assessments aligned with the State's academic content and achievement standards. If the State has adopted alternate achievement standards, children taught to those standards are assessed on those standards.

1999 Regulations (IDEA '97, P.L. 105-17)	2006 Regulations (IDEA '04, P.L. 108-446)
3. States must report, with the same frequency as for nondisabled children, on the number of children with disabilities taking regular and alternate assessments and performance results on those assessments.	3. SEAs must report on the number of children receiving accommodations on regular assessments, the number taking alternate assessments based on alternate standards, and a comparison of performance of children with disabilities with all children, including children with disabilities, on those assessments.
4. Reports must include aggregated data on performance of children with and without disabilities and disaggregated data on performance of children with disabilities.	4. SEAs or LEAs must, to the extent feasible, use universal design principles in developing and administering any assessments.

Participation in Assessments: Under NCLB, States may develop alternate achievement standards for students with significant cognitive disabilities, as defined by each State, as indicated on their IEPs. Students whose instruction is based on alternate achievement standards will take alternate assessments keyed to those standards. There is no limit on the number of students who may take alternate assessments based on alternate standards; however, a cap of up to 1% of those scores may be used in the AYP calculation.

The Department has added another flexibility provision to allow States to develop "modified achievement standards" for children who are "not likely to achieve grade-level proficiency within the school year covered by the student's IEP" (Federal Register, Dec. 15, 2005, p. 74624). A cap of up to 2% of scores on assessments based on modified achievement standards may be used to determine AYP, but there is no limit on the number of students that may be assessed based on modified standards.

Section 300.160, where regulations on participation in assessments will be located, is currently designated as "Reserved." Proposed regulations on modified achievement standards were distributed in December 2005, and the final version will be incorporated in both the IDEA and NCLB regulations. Currently the Department of Education is reviewing and analyzing public comments on the proposed regulations and is expected to issue final regulations early in 2007.

1999 Regulations (IDEA '97, P.L. 105-17)	2006 Regulations (IDEA '04, P.L. 108-446)
Sec. 300.280. Public Hearings Before Adopting State Policies and Procedures. Before adoption of policies and procedures, SEAs must make them publicly available, hold public hearings, and provide opportunity for public comment.	**Sec. 300.165. Public Participation.** Provision is basically the same, with the following addition: States must ensure that opportunity for comment is available to the general public, *including individuals with disabilities and parents of children with disabilities.*

State Advisory Panel

State Advisory Panel

Secs. 300.650; 300. 651. Establishment of Advisory Panels; Membership. States must establish an advisory panel, appointed by the Governor or other authorized individual, for purposes of providing policy guidance on special education and related services. Panel members must include parents of children with disabilities; individuals with disabilities; teachers; representatives of institutions that prepare special education personnel, other State agencies providing or paying for special education services, public charter and private schools, juvenile and adult corrections agencies, and agencies or organizations providing transition services; SEA and LEA officials; and, program administrators.	**Sec. 300.168. Membership.** Provision is the same with the following addition: The list of required members also includes an official responsible for carrying out the McKinney-Vento Homeless Assistance Act and a representative of the State child welfare agency responsible for foster care.

Other Provisions Required for State Eligibility

Other Provisions Required for State Eligibility

Sec. 300.146. Suspension and Expulsion Rates. SEAs must examine data for significant discrepancies in rates of long-term suspensions and expulsions	**Sec. 300.170. Suspension and Expulsion Rates.** Provision is the same with the following addition:

1999 Regulations (IDEA '97, P.L. 105-17)	2006 Regulations (IDEA '04, P.L. 108-446)
among LEAs in the State or as compared to rates for nondisabled students. If discrepancies occur, the SEA reviews and, if appropriate, revises policies and practices related to development and implementation of IEPs, the use of behavioral interventions, and procedural safeguards.	Data must be disaggregated by race and ethnicity.
Access to Instructional Materials. No comparable language.	***Sec. 300.172. Access to Instructional Materials.*** 1. SEAs must adopt the National Instructional Materials Accessibility Standard (NIMAS) to provide instructional materials to blind persons or those with print disabilities. 2. States do not have to coordinate with the National Instructional Materials Access Center (NIMAC), but must assure that they will provide materials to blind or print disabled individuals in a timely manner. 3. SEAs must have a definition of "timely manner," if the State is not coordinating with NIMAC, since the law requires SEAs who do not coordinate to assure provision of instructional materials to blind persons or persons with other print disabilities "in a timely manner." 4. If the SEA chooses to coordinate with NIMAC, it must provide instructional materials to blind persons or other persons with print disabilities in a timely manner.

5. SEAs are responsible for ensuring, in a timely manner, that instructional materials in accessible formats are provided to other children with disabilities who are not included in the definition of "blind persons or other persons with print disabilities" (See explanation below) or who need materials that cannot be produced from NIMAS files.

6. To meet the responsibility to ensure these children are provided materials in a timely manner, SEAs must ensure that LEAs take all reasonable steps to provide materials in accessible formats to children with disabilities who need them at the same time as other children receive instructional materials.

7. In carrying out this section of the regulations, the SEA, to the maximum extent possible, must collaborate with the agency responsible for assistive technology programs.

8. If the SEA coordinates with NIMAC, the State must contract with publishers to provide electronic files of print instructional materials to the NIMAC using the NIMAS or must buy materials in specialized formats.

Access to Instructional Materials. The National Instructional Accessibility Standard (NIMAS) is included in full in Appendix C of the 2006 IDEA regulations. The purpose of the NIMAS is to improve the quality and consistency of print materials that are converted to specialized formats and to make those materials more readily and easily accessible. The process is not intended to provide materials that are universally designed. However, the NIMAS Development Center is examining the need for changes in the NIMAS, including the extent to which they can incorporate universal design features in the future.

Section 674(e) of the statute defines "blind or other persons with print disabilities" by reference to the Library of Congress regulations for "An Act to Provide Books to Blind Adults" (36 CFR 701.6). This definition limits the authority of the NIMAC to provide assistance to SEAs and LEAs in acquiring materials for children who are blind, have visual disabilities, or are unable to read or use standard print materials because of physical limitations and children with reading disabilities resulting from organic dysfunction.

1999 Regulations (IDEA '97, P.L. 105-17)	2006 Regulations (IDEA '04, P.L. 108-446)
Overidentification and Disproportionality. No comparable language.	*Sec. 300.173. Overidentification and Disproportionality.* SEAs must adopt policies and procedures designed to prevent inappropriate identification or disproportionate representation by race and ethnicity of children as children with disabilities.
Prohibition on Mandatory Medication. No comparable language.	*Sec. 300.174. Prohibition on Mandatory Medication.* 1. States shall prohibit SEA and LEA personnel from requiring a child to obtain a prescription for medications covered by the Controlled Substances Act as a condition of school attendance or of receiving an evaluation or special education services. 2. This provision does not prohibit teachers or other school personnel

| | from consulting or sharing classroom observations with parents regarding academic and functional performance, behavior, or the need for an evaluation for special education and related services. |

By-Pass for Children in Private Schools | By-Pass for Children in Private Schools

Secs. 300.484; 300.485. Show Cause Hearing; Decision. These provisions relate to SEAs that were prohibited by State law on the date of the enactment of the 1983 amendments from providing special education for children with disabilities in private schools. In those instances, the U.S. Secretary of Education was empowered to implement a by-pass to provide services to those children, as appropriate. SEAs are given the opportunity, in a hearing, to show cause why a by-pass should not be implemented.

Secs. 300.194; 300.195; 300.198. Show Cause Hearing; Decision; Continuation of a By-Pass. The regulations remain basically the same, with the following additions:

1. If a show cause hearing is requested, the Secretary must notify the SEA, LEA, or other public agency and representatives of private schools that they may be represented by legal counsel and submit oral or written evidence and arguments at the hearing.

2. The Secretary's designee at the hearing has no authority to require or conduct discovery.

3. Within 10 days after the hearing, the designee either indicates that a decision will be issued based on the existing record or requests additional information from the parties.

4. A written decision is issued within 120 days after the hearing record is closed. Each party may submit comments and recommendations on the decision to the Secretary within 30 days of receipt of the decision.

	5. The Secretary continues the by-pass until it is determined that the SEA, LEA, or other agency will meet the requirements to provide services to private school children.

State Administration	**State Administration**

State Administration. No comparable language.	*Sec. 300.199. State Administration.*
	
	1. Each State receiving funds under the IDEA must
	   a. Ensure that any State special education rules, regulations, and policies conform to the purposes of the IDEA.
	   b. Identify in writing to their LEAs and the Secretary any State rules, regulations, or policies that are not required by the federal law.
	   c. Minimize the number of rules, regulations, and policies to which LEAs are subject under the IDEA.
	
	2. State rules, regulations, and policies must support and facilitate district and school improvement focused on enabling children with disabilities to meet State academic achievement standards.

Subpart C–Local Educational Agency Eligibility

1999 Regulations (IDEA '97, P.L. 105-17)

Secs. 300.230; 300.184. Use of Amounts; Excess Cost Requirement.

1. LEAs must provide information to demonstrate that federal funds will be spent in accordance with regulations, will be used only to pay excess costs of providing special education and related services, and will be used to supplement, and not supplant, State, local, and other federal funds.

2. "Excess costs" means cost in excess of the average annual per-pupil expenditure during the preceding school year for an elementary or secondary school student, and must be computed after deducting funds under Part B (IDEA), Title I-Part A or Title VII-Part A (ESEA), and any State or local funds spent on programs that would qualify under those parts.

3. LEAs may not use federal funds to pay for all of the education costs for children with disabilities; however, those funds may be used for all the education costs for children ages 3, 4, 5, 18, 19, 20, or 21, if no local or State funds are available for nondisabled children of those ages.

2006 Regulations (IDEA '04, P.L. 108-446)

Sec. 300.202. Use of Amounts.
Provision has not changed, but the two previous provisions have been consolidated.

1999 Regulations (IDEA '97, P.L. 105-17)	2006 Regulations (IDEA '04, P.L. 108-446)
Secs. 300.231; 300.232. Maintenance of Effort; Exception to Maintenance of Effort.	*Secs. 300.203; 300.204. Maintenance of Effort; Exception to Maintenance of Effort.* Provisions remain the same with the following addition:
1. Except as noted in #2 below, federal funds to LEAs may not be used to reduce the level of expenditures from local funds on educating children with disabilities below the level of the preceding fiscal year.	A reduction in expenditures is allowed if the SEA assumes the costs of a high cost fund previously borne by the LEA.
2. LEAs may reduce their level of expenditures below the previous fiscal year's level if the reduction is attributable to (1) voluntary staff departures where personnel are replaced by lower-salaried staff; (2) enrollment decreases; (3) termination of an obligation to a child with an exceptionally expensive program; or (3) termination of costly expenditures for long-term purchases.	
Sec. 300.233. Treatment of Federal Funds in Certain Fiscal Years.	*Sec. 300.205. Adjustment to Local Fiscal Effort in Certain Fiscal Years.* The provision is changed as follows:
1. In any year where the federal appropriation for Part B exceeds $4.1 billion, the LEA may treat as local funds up to 20% of the federal funds it receives that exceeds the amount received in the previous fiscal year.	1. In any year where the LEA's federal allocation exceeds the previous year's amount, the LEA may reduce its level of expenditures by not more than 50% of the amount of excess.
2. Excess cost requirements do not apply to the amount that may be treated as local funds.	2. If the LEA chooses to reduce its level of expenditure, it must use an amount of local funds equal to that reduction for activities authorized under NCLB.
3. If the SEA determines that an LEA is not meeting requirements of the	

law, the SEA may be prohibit the LEA from utilizing this provision, but only if authorized by State Constitution or State statute.	3. If an SEA determines that an LEA is not able to meet its obligations to provide FAPE or the SEA has taken enforcement action (Subpart F) against the LEA, the LEA will be prohibited from reducing its level of expenditures. 4. Funds spent by the LEA on "early intervening" (Sec. 300.226) shall count toward the maximum amount the LEA may reduce.

Sec. 300.234. Schoolwide Programs Under Title I of the ESEA.

1. LEAs may use Part B funds to carry out schoolwide programs under ESEA, but the amount cannot exceed the amount of those funds received by the LEA that year, divided by the number of children with disabilities in the LEA, and multiplied by the number of children with disabilities in the schoolwide program.

2. Excess cost requirements do not apply to these funds, but all other provisions of the law must be met, including provision of IEP services and all rights and protections.

Sec. 300.206. Schoolwide Programs Under Title I of the ESEA. Provision has not changed.

Statutory Sec. 613(a)(3). Personnel Development. LEAs must ensure that all personnel are appropriately and adequately trained, and as appropriate, will use the State's comprehensive system of personnel development (CSPD).

Sec. 300.207. Personnel Development. This provision, which was previously only in the statute, remains the same, except for the removal of the reference to the State's CSPD has been removed. The CSPD provision was deleted from the statute.

1999 Regulations (IDEA '97, P.L. 105-17)	2006 Regulations (IDEA '04, P.L. 108-446)
Sec. 300.235. Permissive Use of Funds. LEAs may use funds for services and aids that also benefit nondisabled students and for a coordinated service system.	**Sec. 300.208. Permissive Use of Funds.** The Coordinated Services System was deleted from the statute. In addition to using funds for services that also benefit nondisabled student, funds may be used for (1) a coordinated, early intervening educational services system (Sec. 300.226); (2) cost or risk sharing funds, consortia, or cooperatives for high cost special education and related services; and (3) technology for record-keeping, data collection and other case management activities.
Sec. 300.241; 300.312. Treatment of Charter Schools and Their Students; Children with Disabilities in Public Charter Schools.	**Sec. 300.209. Treatment of Charter Schools and Their Students.** Provisions are the same, with the following additions:
1. Charter schools that are public schools of the LEA must serve children with disabilities in the same manner as the LEA's other schools, and the LEA must provide Part B funds just as it does to its other schools. 2. Children with disabilities in public charter schools and their parents have all rights under the law. 3. Charter schools that are LEAs are responsible for meeting the requirements of the law, unless State law assigns the responsibility to another entity. 4. If the charter school is a school of an LEA, the LEA is responsible for ensuring the law's requirements are	1. If the charter school is a school of an LEA, the LEA is responsible for (a) providing funding to the charter school on the same basis provided to its other schools, including proportional distribution based on relative enrollment of children with disabilities, and at the same time funds are distributed to other public schools; and, (b) serving children in the same manner, including providing supplementary and related services on site to the same extent provided to other schools.

1999 Regulations (IDEA '97, P.L. 105-17)	2006 Regulations (IDEA '04, P.L. 108-446)
met, unless State law assigns the responsibility to another entity. 5. If the charter school is neither an LEA nor a school of an LEA, the SEA is responsible for ensuring services or for assigning another entity the responsibility.	
Purchase of Instructional Materials. No comparable language.	*Sec. 300.210. Purchase of Instructional Materials.* This language parallels the language in Sec. 300.172, including an assurance by the LEA that children with disabilities who need materials in accessible formats, but who are not covered under the definition of "blind persons or other persons with print disabilities," will receive those materials in a timely manner. Unlike SEAs in Sec. 300.172, LEAs do not have to coordinate with the NIMAC.
Records Regarding Migratory Children with Disabilities. No comparable language.	*Sec. 300.213. Records Regarding Migratory Children with Disabilities.* LEAs must work with the Secretary to provide electronic exchange among States of health and educational information on migratory children (See NCLB, Sec. 1308).
Sec. 300.244. Coordinated Services System. LEAs may annually use up to 5% of Part B funds to implement a system to improve results for all children, including children with disabilities. Activities allowed under this provision include developing strategies that promote accountability	*Coordinated Services System.* This provision was deleted from the statute.

for results, service coordination and case management, developing interagency financing strategies, and interagency personnel development for personnel working on coordinated services.

Early Intervening Services. No comparable language.

Sec. 300.226. Early Intervening Services (EIS).

1. An LEA annually may use not more than 15% of its Part B funds, in combination with other funds, to develop and implement coordinated early intervening services for students, grades K–12 (focusing on K–3), who are not currently identified as needing special education and related services, but need extra academic and behavioral support to succeed in the general education environment.

2. Activities may include (a) professional development to deliver scientifically based academic and behavioral interventions, and (b) provision of educational and behavioral evaluations, services, and supports, including scientifically based literacy instruction.

3. This provision neither limits nor creates a right to FAPE or can be used to delay evaluation of a child suspected of having a disability.

4. LEAs will report annually to the State on (a) the number of students receiving EIS and (b) the number

1999 Regulations (IDEA '97, P.L. 105-17)	2006 Regulations (IDEA '04, P.L. 108-446)
	receiving EIS who subsequently receive special education and related services during the preceding 2-year period.
	5. These funds may be used for services aligned with NCLB, if funds are used to supplement, and not supplant, NCLB funds.

Early Intervening Services: This provision is specifically targeted to at-risk general education students and has generated some controversy, since IDEA funds will be used for students who are not currently identified as needing special education and related services. A number of school districts already use systems whereby struggling students receive classroom interventions of varying levels of intensity over a period of time. If students are not successful after a series of these interventions, they may be referred for evaluation for special education and related services.

LEAs are required to report on students served in this program for two years to determine if this program reduces the number of referrals for special education and related services. The two-year period applies to the two years after the child has received these services. (Conf. Report, p. 199)

Secs. 300.245–300.250. School-Based Improvement Plan. LEAs may use federal funds to permit schools to implement school-based improvement plans to improve educational and transitional results for children with and without disabilities.	*School-Based Improvement Plan.* This provision was deleted from the statute.
Secs. 300.360; 300.361. Use of LEA Allocation for Direct Services; Nature and Location of Services.	*Sec. 300.227. Direct Services by the SEA.* Provisions have not changed.
1. The SEA must provide services directly to children for whom an LEA or other State agency is	

64

responsible if the SEA determines the LEA or agency (a) has not provided information to establish its eligibility; (b) is unable to provide programs meeting FAPE requirements; (c) is unable or unwilling to consolidate with other LEAs to provide programs; or, (d) has one or more children best served by a regional or State program.

2. If an LEA chooses not to apply for Part B funds, the SEA must use those funds to ensure children in that LEA receive services; and, if those funds aren't sufficient, the SEA may use other funding sources.

3. The SEA may provide services directly, by contract, or through other arrangements in the manner and at a location it deems appropriate, consistent with LRE.

4. Excess cost requirements do not apply to the SEA.

Sec. 300.576. Disciplinary Information.

1. LEAs may be required to include in a child's records a statement of current or previous disciplinary actions and transmit the statement to the same extent disciplinary information is included in and transmitted with records of nondisabled children.

2. Statements may include descriptions of the behavior that required

Sec. 300.229. Disciplinary Information.

Provision has not changed.

disciplinary action, the action taken, and other information relevant to the child's safety and the safety of others involved with the child.

3. If the State adopts this policy and the child transfers schools, records transmitted must include the current IEP and the disciplinary statement.

State Agency Flexibility. No comparable language.

Sec. 300.230. SEA Flexibility.

1. In any year where the State's Part B allotment exceeds the amount received the previous year, and, if the State in school year 2003–04 or any subsequent school year pays or reimburses all LEAs for 100% of the non-federal share of special education and related services, the SEA may reduce the level of expenditures from State sources by not more than 50% of the amount of excess.

2. If the Secretary determines the State cannot meet the requirements of the law and needs assistance or intervention (See Subpart F), the Secretary must prohibit the State from using this authority.

3. If the State uses this authority, the SEA shall use funds from State sources in an amount equal to the reduction to support activities authorized under NCLB or to support need-based or teacher higher education programs.

Subpart D—Evaluations, Eligibility Determinations, Individualized Education Programs, and Educational Placements

1999 Regulations (IDEA '97, P.L. 105-17)	2006 Regulations (IDEA '04, P.L. 108-446)
Parental Consent	**Parental Consent**
Sec. 300.505. Parental Consent.	*Sec. 300.300. Parental Consent.*

1999 Regulations (IDEA '97, P.L. 105-17)

Parental Consent

Sec. 300.505. Parental Consent.

1. Informed parental consent must be obtained before conducting an initial evaluation or reevaluation and before initial provision of special education and related services.

2. Consent for initial evaluation may not be construed as consent for initial placement.

3. Consent is not required before (a) reviewing existing data as part of an evaluation or reevaluation; or, (b) giving a test that is given to all children, unless consent is required of all parents.

4. If parents refuse consent for initial evaluation or reevaluation, the LEA may use due process procedures or mediation to continue to pursue the evaluation.

5. Consent for reevaluation is not required, if parents failed to respond after documented reasonable measures were taken by the LEA to obtain consent.

6. States may require consent for other services and activities, if procedures are in place to provide FAPE even if parents refuse to consent.

2006 Regulations (IDEA '04, P.L. 108-446)

Parental Consent

Sec. 300.300. Parental Consent.

Regulations include the following changes and additions:

1. For initial evaluation,
   a. The LEA must make reasonable efforts to obtain informed consent from the parent.
   b. If the parent of a child enrolled or seeking to be enrolled in public school does not provide consent for initial evaluation or fails to respond to a request to provide consent, the LEA may, but is not required to, pursue the evaluation using the procedural safeguards procedures.
   c. The LEA does not violate its obligation under child find or initial evaluation requirements if it declines to pursue the evaluation.
   d. If the child is a ward of the State and is not residing with the parent, the LEA is not required to obtain informed parental consent if (a) despite reasonable efforts, the parent cannot be found; (b) the parent's rights have been terminated; or, (c) the parent's rights to make educational decisions have been given to another party appointed by a judge to represent the child.

67

7. Parents' refusal to consent to one service or activity may not be used to deny the parents or child any other service, benefit, or activity under the law.

2. For initial provision of special education and related services,
   a. The LEA must make reasonable efforts to obtain informed parental consent for initial provision of special education and related services.
   b. If the parent fails to respond or refuses to consent to services, the LEA may not use the procedural safeguards procedures (including mediation or due process) to obtain a ruling that services may be provided.
   c. The LEA does not violate its obligation to provide FAPE if parents refuse consent for services, nor must the LEA convene an IEP meeting or develop an IEP.

3. For reevaluation,
   a. If the parent refuses to consent to reevaluation, the LEA may, but is not required to, pursue the reevaluation using the procedural safeguards procedures.
   b. The LEA does not violate its obligation under child find or evaluation requirements if it declines to pursue the evaluation or the reevaluation.

4. For children who are home-schooled or parentally placed in private schools,
   a. If the parent does not provide consent for initial evaluation or reevaluation, or the parent fails

	to respond to a request for consent, the LEA may not use the due process procedures.
	b. The LEA is not required to consider the child as eligible for services under the "private school" provisions (Secs. 300.132–300.144).
	5. To meet the "reasonable efforts" requirements, the LEA must document its attempts to obtain parental consent using the procedures in the IEP section [Sec. 300.322(d)].

Evaluations and Reevaluations	**Evaluations and Reevaluations**
Secs. 300.531; 300.532. Initial Evaluation; Evaluation Procedures. LEAs shall conduct a full and individual initial evaluation to determine if the child is a child with a disability and to determine the educational needs of the child before initial provision of special education and related services.	***Sec. 300.301. Initial Evaluations.*** Additions include:
	1. Parents or the SEA, other state agency, or the LEA may request an initial evaluation.
	2. The evaluation must be conducted within 60 days of receiving parental consent for evaluation, or, if the State has an established timeframe for evaluation, that timeframe is used.
	3. The time frame does not apply if:
	a. The child enrolls in a new school after the 60-day period has begun and before the child's previous school has made an eligibility determination, but only if the new school is making sufficient progress to ensure prompt completion of the

	evaluation and parents and the new LEA agree to a specific time for completing the evaluation. b. The parent repeatedly fails or refuses to bring the child for evaluation.
Screening for Instructional Purposes is Not Evaluation. No comparable language.	*Sec. 300.302. Screening for Instructional Purposes is Not Evaluation.* Screening of a student by a teacher or specialist to determine instructional strategies shall not be considered an evaluation for eligibility for special education and related services.
Secs. 300.321; 300.536. Reevaluations. LEAs must ensure that children are reevaluated and the results of the reevaluation are addressed in revising the IEP. A reevaluation must be conducted if conditions warrant or if the child's parent or teacher requests a reevaluation, but a reevaluation must be conducted at least once every three years.	*Sec. 300.303. Reevaluations.* Changes and additions include: 1. A reevaluation must be conducted if the LEA determines that the child's educational or related services needs, including improved academic achievement and functional performance, warrant a reevaluation. 2. A reevaluation may be conducted not more than once a year, unless the parents and the LEA agree otherwise, and must be conducted at least once every 3 years, unless parents and the LEA agree that is unnecessary.

Initial Evaluation and Reevaluation: The law clarifies that both parents and agency personnel may request an initial evaluation and establishes a time frame within which the evaluation must be completed. The law provides that school districts may utilize the procedural safeguards procedures to override the parents' lack of consent to initial evaluation or reevaluation; however, they are not required to pursue the evaluation or reevaluation using those procedures. In addition, parentally placed private school and home schooled children with disabilities may not be given an initial evaluation or be reevaluated if parents do not provide consent.

The law also prohibits school districts from providing services without parental consent. In the past, school districts could use the due process procedures to provide services even without parental consent, but the new provisions bar districts from using those procedures for this purpose.

Note also that a new federal time line is included in this section. However, if the State has an established time line—whether shorter or longer—that time line will be used. The regulatory discussion indicates the Department's belief that congressional intent is to allow States to make their own determinations of the appropriate time frame for evaluations based on particular State circumstances.

1999 Regulations (IDEA '97, P.L. 105-17)	2006 Regulations (IDEA '04, P.L. 108-446)
Secs. 300.503; 300.532. Prior Notice; Evaluation Procedures.	*Sec. 300.304. Evaluation Procedures.* Changes and additions include:
1. LEAs must provide notice to parents describing any evaluation procedures they propose to conduct.	1. Assessments must be provided and administered in the child's native language or other communication mode "and in the form most likely to yield accurate information on what the child knows and can do academically, developmentally, and functionally. . . ."
2. In conducting the evaluation, the LEA must (a) use a variety of assessment tools, including information provided by parents; (b) not use any single procedure as the sole criterion for determining eligibility; and, (c) use technically sound instruments to assess cognitive, behavioral, physical, and developmental factors.	2. Assessments of a child who transfers to another school district during the school year are coordinated between prior and subsequent schools for expeditious completion of evaluation.
3. Other requirements: a. Tests must be validated for the purpose for which they are used and administered by trained personnel.	

b. If a test is given under non-standard conditions, the evaluation report must include a description of the variance from standard conditions.

c. Evaluation materials or the administration of the evaluation must not be racially or culturally discriminatory.

d. Tests must be administered in the child's native language or other mode of communication, unless not feasible to do so.

e. Materials and procedures used to assess children with limited English proficiency must measure the extent to which the child needs special education and related services, rather than measuring the child's English language skills.

f. Children must be assessed in all areas of suspected disability.

g. Tests must include tests to assess specific areas of educational need and not just those designed to provide a single intelligence quotient.

h. Tests administered to children with impaired sensory, manual, or speaking skills must reflect whatever the test is measuring, rather than reflecting those impairments.

i. The evaluation must be comprehensive enough to identify all of the child's special education and related services needs.

Secs. 300.533; 300.534.; Determination of Needed Evaluation Data; Determination of Eligibility.	***Sec. 300.305. Additional Requirements for Evaluations and Reevaluations.*** Additions include:

Secs. 300.533; 300.534.; Determination of Needed Evaluation Data; Determination of Eligibility.

1. As part of the initial evaluation, if appropriate, and any reevaluation, the IEP team and other qualified professionals, as appropriate, must
   a. Review existing data, including evaluations and information from the parents, current classroom assessments and observations, and observations by teachers and related services personnel; and,
   b. Based on the data review and input from parents, decide what other data, if any, are needed to determine (1) whether the child has a particular category of disability or, in a reevaluation, continues to have a disability; (2) present levels of performance and educational need; (3) whether the child needs services, or in case of a reevaluation, continues to need services; and (4) whether any additions or modifications to services are needed to enable the child to meet IEP goals and to participate, as appropriate, in the general curriculum.

2. The data review may be conducted without a meeting.

3. If additional data are needed, the LEA must administer tests and evaluation materials identified by the group.

Sec. 300.305. Additional Requirements for Evaluations and Reevaluations. Additions include:

1. Review of existing data includes "current classroom-based, *local, or State* assessments. . . ."

2. Data are needed to determine "present levels of *achievement and related developmental needs. . . .*"

3. The IEP team and other qualified professionals, as appropriate, may determine that additional data are not needed to determine whether the child continues to be a child with a disability *"and to determine the child's educational needs. . . ."*

4. Parents may request an assessment to determine whether the child continues to be a child with a disability *"and to determine the child's educational needs. . . ."*

5. For a child whose eligibility terminates due to graduation with a regular high school diploma or exceeds the State's age for provision of FAPE, the LEA must provide the child with a summary of academic achievement and functional performance, which must include recommendations on how to assist the child in meeting postsecondary goals.

4. If additional data are not needed to determine whether the child continues to be a child with a disability, the LEA must notify the parents (a) of that determination and the reasons for it; and, (b) of parents' right to request an assessment to determine, for purposes of services, whether the child continues to be a child with a disability.

5. The LEA is not required to conduct an assessment in 4(b) above unless parents request it.

6. An evaluation is not necessary to determine if a child is no longer a child with a disability before (a) the termination of a child's eligibility for services due to graduation with a regular high school diploma; or, (b) exceeding the State age of eligibility for FAPE.

Secs. 300.534; 300.535. Determination of Eligibility; Procedures for Determining Eligibility and Placement.

1. Upon completion of the evaluation, a group of qualified professionals and the parent must determine if the child is a "child with a disability," and a copy of the evaluation report and documentation of eligibility must be provided to the parent.

2. A child may not be determined eligible if the determinant factor is (a) lack of instruction in reading or math or limited English proficiency;

Sec. 300.306. Determination of Eligibility. Additions include:

1. The group determines whether the child is a child with a disability and the child's *educational needs.*

2. The determinant factor in deciding eligibility must not be *lack of appropriate instruction in reading, including the "essential components of reading instruction"* as defined in NCLB, Sec. 1208(3) ("Reading First" program), lack of appropriate math instruction, or limited English proficiency.

and, (b) the child does not otherwise meet the eligibility criteria.	
3. In interpreting evaluation data for determination of eligibility and educational needs, LEAs must (a) use information from a variety of sources, including aptitude and achievement tests, parent input, teacher recommendations, physical condition, social or cultural background, and adaptive behavior; and, (b) ensure that information from these sources is documented and carefully considered.	
4. If it is determined that the child has a disability and requires special education and related services, an IEP must be developed that meets the requirements of the law.	

Additional Procedures for Identifying Children with Specific Learning Disabilities (SLD)	Additional Procedures for Identifying Children with Specific Learning Disabilities (SLD)

Specific Learning Disabilities. No comparable language.	***Sec. 300.307. Specific Learning Disabilities.*** A State must adopt criteria, which LEAs are required to use, for determining whether a child has a specific learning disability. Those criteria
	
	    a. Must not require the use of a severe discrepancy between intellectual ability and achievement;
	
	    b. Must permit the use of a process based on the child's response to

75

	scientific, research-based intervention; and,
	c. May permit the use of other alternative research-based procedures.

Sec. 300.540. Additional Team Members. The determination of whether a child suspected of having an SLD is a child with a disability under the law must be made by the parents and a team of qualified professionals which must include (a) the child's regular teacher, or, if the child does not have a regular teacher, a regular classroom teacher qualified to teach a child of that age; or, for a child under school age, a person qualified by the SEA to teach a child of that age; and, (b) at least one person qualified to conduct individual diagnostic tests, such as a school psychologist, speech-language pathologist, or remedial reading teacher.	*Sec. 300.308. Additional Group Members.* Provision has not changed.

Sec. 300.541. Criteria for Determining the Existence of a Specific Learning Disability.	*Sec. 300.309. Determining the Existence of a Specific Learning Disability.* The regulation is changed as follows:
1. A team may determine that a child has a specific learning disability if: a. The child does not achieve commensurate with age and ability levels, if provided with learning experiences appropriate for age and ability level, in one or more of the following areas: oral expression, listening comprehension, written expression, basic reading skill, reading	1. The group may determine that a child has a specific learning disability if: a. The child does not achieve adequately for the child's age or to meet State-approved grade-level standards in one or more of the listed areas when provided with learning experiences and instruction appropriate for the child's age or State-approved

comprehension, math calculation, and math reasoning; and,

b. The team finds a severe discrepancy between achievement and intellectual ability in one or more of the listed areas.

2. The team may not identify a child as having a specific learning disability if the severe discrepancy between achievement and ability is primarily the result of a visual, hearing, or motor impairment; mental retardation; emotional disturbance; or environmental, cultural, or economic disadvantage.

grade-level standards. [The list remains the same, with the addition of "reading fluency skills" and a change from mathematics "reasoning" to mathematics "problem solving."]

b. (1) The child does not make sufficient progress to meet age or State-approved grade-level standards in one or more of the listed areas when using a process based on the child's response to scientific, research-based intervention; or, (2) The child exhibits a pattern of strengths and weaknesses in performance, achievement, or both, relative to age, State-approved grade-level standards, or intellectual development, determined by the group to be relevant to the identification of a specific learning disability based on appropriate assessments; and,

c. The group determines that findings under (a) or (b) are not primarily the result of a visual, hearing, or motor disability; mental retardation; emotional disturbance; cultural factors; environmental or economic disadvantage; or limited English proficiency.

2. To ensure that underachievement in a child suspected of having a specific learning disability is not due to lack of appropriate instruction in

reading or math, the group must consider as part of the evaluation:

a. Data demonstrating that prior to, or as part of, the referral process, the child received appropriate instruction in regular education settings provided by qualified personnel; and,

b. Data-based documentation provided to the child's parents of repeated assessments of achievement at reasonable intervals that reflect formal assessment of the child's progress during instruction.

3. The LEA must promptly request parental consent to evaluate the child for special education and related services,

a. If, prior to a referral, the child has not made adequate progress after an appropriate period of time when provided with appropriate instruction by qualified personnel; and,

b. Whenever a child is referred for an evaluation.

Sec. 300.542. Observation. At least one team member other than the child's regular teacher must observe the child's academic performance in the regular classroom. For a child who is out of school or not yet school age, the member must observe the child in an environment appropriate to the child's age.

Sec. 300.310. Observation. Additions include:

1. The LEA must ensure that the child is observed in the child's learning environment to document academic performance and behavior in the areas of difficulty. (**Note:** deleted reference to a team member "other than the child's regular teacher.")

	2. In determining whether the child has a specific learning disability, the group must decide to use information (a) from an observation of routine classroom instruction and monitoring of the child's performance before the referral for evaluation, or (b) must conduct observations.
Sec. 300.543. Written Report. Documentation from the team's determination of eligibility must include whether the child has a specific learning disability; the basis for that determination; the relevant behavior observed; the relationship of that behavior to academic functioning; educationally relevant medical findings, if any; whether there is a severe discrepancy between achievement and ability that is not correctable without special education and related services; and, the team's determination regarding effects of environmental, cultural, or economic disadvantage.	*Sec. 300.311. Specific Documentation for the Eligibility Determination.* New regulations (1) eliminate the requirement of a severe discrepancy between achievement and ability; and, (2) require that documentation include statements about the group's determinations under Sec. 300.309, plus a statement about the following: If the child has participated in a process assessing the child's response to scientific, research-based interventions, a. The instructional strategies used and student-centered data collected; b. Documentation that the child's parents were notified about: (1) State policies on the amount and type of student performance data to be collected and the general education services to be provided; (2) Strategies for increasing the child's rate of learning; and, (3) The parents' right to request an evaluation.

Evaluation Procedure/Specific Learning Disabilities: The IQ-discrepancy model has always been quite controversial, particularly in recent years as over 50% of all students with disabilities receiving services under the IDEA are identified as having specific learning disabilities. The model uses a severe discrepancy between the student's intellectual ability, as measured by an IQ test, and actual achievement and performance as the primary indicator of a learning disability.

The controversy has arisen for several reasons. First, the law has never required the use of an IQ-discrepancy "formula" as the sole determinant for eligibility, and, in fact, requires the use of a variety of assessment tools and strategies to make a determination of eligibility under any disability category. Despite this requirement, some school districts have adopted this model as the sole criterion for determining specific learning disabilities. Second, a broad range of researchers and advocates believe that using an IQ-discrepancy formula as the sole criterion has resulted in over- and misidentification of learning disabilities and does not account for other possible factors resulting in academic failure, such as poor instruction or lack of appropriate interventions.

These provisions clarify that school districts do not have to take into consideration whether the child has a severe discrepancy between ability and achievement to determine a child eligible for special education and related services under the category of specific learning disabilities. The regulations explain that the LEA *must not require* the use of a "severe discrepancy between achievement and intellectual ability." In addition, the LEA *must permit* the use of a scientific, research-based intervention (known generically as "response to intervention" or RTI) and *may permit* the use of other research-based procedures. In the regulatory discussion, the Department notes that "States are free to prohibit the use of a discrepancy model," since States are responsible for developing criteria to determine whether a child is a child with a disability, including criteria for specific learning disabilities.

RTI is a multi-tiered process through which a series of interventions of increasing intensity are used to address learning difficulties. The process is implemented with children in general education, culminating for some non-responsive students in an evaluation for special education and related services. RTI is not a substitute for a comprehensive evaluation for special education eligibility, nor can data from an RTI process be used as the sole determinant of eligibility for special education. Rather, data from an RTI process may be used as one component of the evaluation. For children who show progress under these interventions, school personnel should carefully evaluate whether or not the child has a true learning disability or whether academic difficulties are due to lack of proper instruction or other factors.

1999 Regulations (IDEA '97, P.L. 105-17)	2006 Regulations (IDEA '04, P.L. 108-446)
Individualized Education Programs (IEP)	**Individualized Education Programs (IEP)**

Secs. 300.340; 300.346; 300.347. Definitions Related to IEPs; Development, Review, and Revision of IEP; Content of IEP.	*Sec. 300.320. Definition of Individualized Education Program.*

1. "IEP" means a written statement for a child with a disability that is developed, reviewed, and revised in a meeting, in accordance with Secs. 300.340–300.350.	1. The new statute and regulations have deleted:
	  a. Benchmarks or short-term objectives: Retained only for children who take alternate assessments aligned to alternate achievement standards.
	  b. Transition requirement at age 14.

2. The IEP must include statements of the following:
  a. Present levels of educational performance, including how the disability affects involvement and progress in the general curriculum, or, for preschoolers, how the disability affects participation in appropriate activities.
  b. Measurable annual goals, including benchmarks or short-term objectives, related to (1) meeting the child's needs to enable the child to be involved and progress in the general curriculum, or, for preschoolers, as appropriate, to participate in appropriate activities; and, (2) meeting the child's other educational needs resulting from the disability.
  c. Special education and related services and supplementary aids and services the child needs to (1) advance toward annual goals, (2) be involved and progress in
	2. Changes and additions to IEP content requirements are as follows:
	  a. Present levels of *academic achievement and functional* performance.
	  b. Measurable annual goals, *including academic and functional goals.*
	  c. When periodic progress reports will be provided, e.g., *quarterly or other periodic reports issued at the same time as regular report cards.*
	  d. Special education and related services and supplementary aids and services, *based on peer-reviewed research to the extent practicable.*
	  e. Appropriate accommodations necessary to measure the child's academic achievement and functional performance on state or district assessments.
	  f. If the IEP team determines the child should take an alternate assessment, why the child can't

the general curriculum and participate in extracurricular and other nonacademic activities, and (3) be educated and participate with other children with disabilities and nondisabled children in the activities described in this section.

d. Explanation of the extent to which the child will not participate with nondisabled children in the regular classroom.

e. Individual modifications in administration of State or district-wide assessments necessary for the child to participate in the assessments, and, if an assessment is not appropriate, why it is not appropriate and how the child will be assessed.

f. Projected date services and modifications will begin, and frequency and location of those services and modifications.

g. How (1) progress toward annual goals and sufficiency of progress to achieve goals by year's end will be measured; and, (b) how the parents will be informed (e.g., through periodic report cards), at least as often as parents of nondisabled children are informed of their child's progress.

h. Transition Services: (1) beginning at age 14 (or younger, if the IEP

participate in the regular assessment and why the particular alternate assessment selected is appropriate.

3. Transition Services: Beginning not later than the first IEP in effect when the student is 16, or younger if the IEP team determines it appropriate, and updated annually, the IEP must include:

a. "Appropriate measurable postsecondary goals based on age appropriate transition assessments related to training, education, employment, and where appropriate, independent skills."

b. Transition services, including courses of study, needed to assist in reaching goals.

4. No additional information is required to be included in a child's IEP beyond what is explicitly mentioned in this section.

team determines) and updated annually, transition service needs, focusing on courses of study; and, (2) at age 16 (or younger, if the IEP team determines), transition services, including interagency responsibilities.	
i. Information regarding transfer of rights at the age of majority.	
3. The IEP team is not required to include information under one component of the IEP that is already found under another component.	

Definition of Individualized Education Program. One of the major changes on the IEP is the elimination of benchmarks or short-term objectives, except in the instance of children who take alternate assessments based on alternate achievement standards. The regulatory discussion indicates that short-term objectives were intended originally to aid parents in following their child's progress toward meeting the IEP goals. The Department has indicated that a State could continue to require short-term objectives or benchmarks, but would have to identify to its LEAs and the Secretary that the State requirements goes beyond federal law (See Sec. 300.199).

The regulations also require that the team decides the appropriate special education and related services and supplementary aids and services, *based on peer-reviewed research to the extent practicable.* "Peer-reviewed research" is not defined in the regulations. However, the regulatory discussion indicates that the term generally refers to research reviewed by qualified independent researchers to ensure that the information meets accepted standards in the field. On the face of it, this requirement could add an additional, and possibly unnecessary, burden on the IEP team, since the team itself must be comprised of individuals with a high degree of expertise in educating children with disabilities.

In 1997, Congress added a requirement that transition planning begin at age 14. This requirement was deleted in the 2004 amendments, and instead, requiring transition planning to begin at the first IEP meeting after the child turns 16. However, the regulations allow the team discretion to begin transition planning before age 16, if they believe it is appropriate. As with short-term objectives, a State regulation that requires transition planning before age 16 would have to be disseminated in writing to the LEAs and the Secretary, indicating that the rule exceeds federal law in this area.

1999 Regulations (IDEA '97, P.L. 105-17)	2006 Regulations (IDEA '04, P.L. 108-446)
Sec. 300.344. IEP Team.	*Sec. 300.321. IEP Team.*
1. The IEP team must include the parents; at least one of the child's regular education teachers (if the child is, or may be, participating in the regular education environment); at least one special education teacher, or if appropriate, at last one special education provider; an LEA representative who is qualified to provide or supervise provision of services and is knowledgeable about general education curriculum and about the available LEA resources; a person who can interpret instructional implications of evaluation results (may be one of the other team members); at the discretion of parents or the LEA, other individuals with special knowledge or expertise about the child (as determined by the inviting party); and, if appropriate, the child.	1. Team members remain the same, with the following addition to "transition services participants": a. The purpose of the meeting will be consideration of *postsecondary goals* and transition services needed to reach those goals. b. *To the extent appropriate, with the consent of the parents or a child who has reached the age of majority,* the LEA must invite a representative of any participating agency likely to be responsible for providing or paying for transition services.
2. Transition meeting: (a) The child must be invited if the team will discuss transition, and, if the child does not attend, the LEA must ensure that the child's preferences and interests are considered. (b) Representatives of other	2. IEP Team Attendance: a. A team member is not required to attend a part or all of a meeting if the parents and LEA agree, in writing, that the member's attendance is not necessary, because the member's curriculum area or related service will not be modified or discussed. b. A team member may be excused from part or all of a meeting when his/her curriculum area or

84

agencies likely to be responsible for providing or paying for transition services must be invited, and, if the agency does not send a representative, the LEA must take other steps to obtain input. *IEP Team Attendance.* No comparable language.	related service is being modified or discussed, if parents, in writing, and the LEA consent to the excusal, and the member submits written input to the parents and the team before the meeting. 3. For a child who was previously served under Part C, at the parent's request, the Part C service coordinator or other Part C representatives must be invited to the initial IEP meeting to assist in smooth transition of services.

IEP Team. The proposed regulations on "excusal," allowing certain IEP team members to be excused from attendance, generated significant comment. The Department notes that the intention in allowing team members to be excused is to provide parents additional flexibility in scheduling meetings and to avoid delaying meetings if certain team members are unable to be present. Parents must provide informed written consent if a team member whose curriculum area will be discussed is excused. The intention is not that there will be routine excusals, rather that there be a careful decision about whether or not the person's input in person would be so critical as to dictate that rescheduling the meeting would be the better judgment.

Allowing parents to have a Part C representative at an initial IEP meeting may provide a smoother transition for children moving into the Preschool program. The Part C and Preschool programs differ in the types of services provided, as well as duration, frequency, and location of services. Program representatives should help parents to understand these changes as an IEP is developed.

Sec. 300.345. Parent Participation.	*Sec. 300.322. Parent Participation.*

Sec. 300.345. Parent Participation.

1. LEAs must take steps to ensure parents are at each IEP meeting or afforded an opportunity to participate.

2. Notice of meetings must include meeting logistics and attendees and that parents are allowed to invite other individuals with knowledge or special expertise to the meeting.

3. For meetings related to transition, the notice must include the purpose of the meeting, an invitation for the child to attend, and identification of representatives of other agencies who will be invited.

4. If neither parent can attend, LEAs must use other methods to ensure parent participation, including conference calls.

5. Meetings may be conducted without a parent if the LEA cannot convince parents to attend. LEAs must document attempts to arrange a mutually agreeable time and place, such as records of phone calls and results of calls; correspondence and any responses; and, home or workplace visits and results.

6. LEAs must do whatever is necessary to ensure parents understand the IEP meeting proceedings, including arranging interpreters for parents with

Sec. 300.322. Parent Participation.
Additions include:

1. Meeting notices must include information about possible participation of the Part C service coordinator or other Part C representative at an initial IEP meeting for a child previously served under Part C.

2. For a transition meeting, the notice must indicate that the purpose of the meeting is to consider postsecondary goals and transition services.

deafness or whose native language is not English.

7. LEAs must give parents a copy of the IEP at no cost to the parents.

Sec. 300.342. When IEPs Must Be in Effect.

1. LEAs must have an IEP in effect at the beginning of the school year for each child with a disability.

2. LEAs must ensure that IEPs are (a) in effect before provision of services; (b) implemented as soon as possible after development; and, (c) accessible to each regular and special education teacher and related services provider responsible for implementation.

3. Teachers and providers in 2(c) must be informed of their specific responsibilities for implementation and of accommodations, modifications, and supports the child must receive.

4. For children aged 3–5 (or, at the SEA's discretion, a 2-year-old who will turn 3 during the school year), the LEA may use an Individualized Family Service Plan (IFSP) if, after an explanation of the differences between IEPs and IFSPs, parents and LEA agree and the parents provide written informed consent.

Sec. 300.323. When IEPs Must be in Effect. Additions include:

1. In considering an IFSP for children aged 3–5, regulations include new IFSP content: "an educational component that promotes school readiness and incorporates pre-literacy, language, and numeracy skills."

2. Children transferring schools within and outside the State:

   a. If a child transfers to another school district *within the State* during the school year, the new LEA must provide FAPE, including services comparable to the previous IEP, in consultation with the parents, until the previous IEP is adopted or a new IEP is developed, adopted, and implemented.

   b. If a child transfers to a school in another State during the school year, the new LEA must provide FAPE, including services comparable to the previous IEP, in consultation with the parents, until a new evaluation is conducted, if deemed necessary, and a new IEP is developed, adopted, and implemented.

    c. When a child transfers, (1) the receiving school must take reasonable steps to promptly obtain records, including the IEP and other documents related to providing special education and related services; and, (2) the sending school must take reasonable steps to respond promptly to a request to send the child's records.

Sec. 300.346. Development, Review, and Revision of IEP.

1. In developing an IEP, teams must consider (a) the child's strengths and parents' concern for enhancing the child's education; (b) results of the initial or most recent evaluation; and, (c) as appropriate, performance results on any general State or district-wide assessments.

2. Special factors: (a) for children whose behavior impedes their learning or that of others, consider, if appropriate, strategies and supports to address the behavior; (b) for children with limited English proficiency, consider language needs; (c) for children who are blind or visually impaired, provide Braille instruction, unless determined not appropriate; (d) for all children, consider communication needs, and, for children who are deaf or hard of hearing, language and communication

Sec. 300.324. Development, Review and Revision of IEP. Additions include:

1. In developing the IEP, the team must consider the child's academic, developmental, and functional needs.

2. If changes are made to the IEP after the annual IEP meeting,
   a. The parents and the LEA may agree not to convene a meeting to make those changes, but rather may develop a document to amend or modify the IEP.
   b. If amendments or modifications are made without a meeting, the IEP team must be informed of the changes.
   c. Upon request, parents must be given a copy of the amended IEP.

3. The LEA, to the extent possible, must encourage consolidation of reevaluation and other IEP team meetings.

needs; and, (e) for all children, consider whether they need assistive technology devices and services.

3. In meetings to review, and, as appropriate, revise IEPs, teams must consider the factors in #1 and #2 above.

4. If, in considering the special factors (#2 above), the team determines the child needs a particular device or service (including interventions, accommodations, or modifications) to receive FAPE, the team must include a statement to that effect on the IEP.

5. The child's regular education teacher, as an IEP team member, must, to the extent appropriate, participate in development, review, and revision of the IEP, including assisting to determine (a) appropriate behavioral interventions and strategies; and, (b) supplementary aids and services, program modifications, or supports for staff.

Sec. 300.349. Private School Placements by Public Agencies.

1. LEAs must (a) conduct a meeting and develop an IEP before placing children in, or referring children to, private schools or facilities; (b) ensure private school/facility representatives attend the meeting, and, if they cannot attend, ensure participation through alternate methods, e.g., conference calls.

Sec. 300.325. Private School Placements by Public Agencies.
Provision has not changed.

2. After the child enters the private school/facility, (a) meetings to review and revise the IEP may be initiated and conducted by the private school/facility at the LEA's discretion; and, (b) the LEA must ensure parents and an LEA representative are involved in decisions about the IEP and agree to any proposed changes before they are implemented.

3. The SEA and LEA remain responsible for compliance with the law, even if the IEP is implemented by a private school or facility.

Sec. 300.501(c). Parent Involvement in Placement Decisions. LEAs must ensure that parents of the child with a disability are members of any group that make decisions on the child's educational placement.

Sec. 300.327. Educational Placements. Provision has not changed.

Sec. 300.345; 300.501. Parent Participation in Meetings. If parents cannot attend IEP meetings or meetings where placement decisions are made, the LEA must use alternate means to ensure their participation, e.g., conference calls or video conferencing.

Sec. 300.328. Alternative Means of Meeting Participation. Provision has been changed, as follows:

In conducting IEP and placement meetings and in carrying out administrative matters, e.g., scheduling, exchange of witness lists and status conferences, the LEA and parents may agree to use alternative means of meeting participation, such as video conferences and conference calls.

Multi-Year IEP Demonstration. No comparable language.

Sec. 614(d)(5). Multi-Year IEP Demonstration.

1. Authorizes 15-State pilot program for an optional multi-year IEP (not to exceed 3 years). The Secretary will report to Congress within 2 years on the effectiveness of the pilot and provide any recommendations for broader implementation.

2. The program must be optional to parents and requires informed consent.

3. The IEP must include (a) measurable goals to enable the child to make progress in the general education curriculum and meet other needs that coincide with natural transition points (preschool to elementary; elementary to middle; middle to secondary; secondary to postsecondary, but in no case longer than 3 years); and, (b) measurable annual goals for determining progress toward meeting academic goals.

4. Review and revision of IEPs must include a review at natural transition points and, in years other than natural transition points, an annual review to determine current progress and whether goals are being met.

5. The IEP must be amended, as appropriate, to allow continued progress toward goals.

| | 6. The LEA must ensure a more thorough review within 30 days if the team determines the child is not making sufficient progress toward meeting goals. |
| | 7. At the parents' request, the team must conduct a review of the IEP rather than or subsequent to an annual review. |

Multi-Year IEP: This pilot is another attempt to address excessive paperwork burdens by streamlining the number of IEP meetings and revisions to the document. Districts and parents will most likely find that a multi-year IEP is more appropriate for children with mild to moderate disabilities, rather than those who receive multiple services that may require more frequent review of the IEP. There are no accompanying regulations, as this is a pilot program.

Subpart E—Procedural Safeguards

1999 Regulations (IDEA '97, P.L. 105-17)	2006 Regulations (IDEA '04, P.L. 108-446)
Due Process Procedures for Parents and Children	**Due Process Procedures for Parents and Children**
Sec. 300.501. Opportunity to Examine Records; Parent Participation in Meetings.	*Sec. 300.501. Opportunity to Examine Records; Parent Participation in Meetings.* Provision has not changed.
1. Parents must have an opportunity to inspect and review all education records and participate in meetings regarding identification, evaluation, educational placement, and provision of FAPE.	

2. LEAs must provide notice (Sec. 300.345) to ensure parents have an opportunity to participate in meetings under #1 above.

3. "Meetings" do not include (a) informal or unscheduled conversations among staff and on issues such as teaching methodology, lesson plans, or coordination of service provision, if those issues are not addressed in the IEP; (b) LEA staff's preparatory activities to develop proposals or responses to parents' proposals to be discussed at a later meeting.

4. LEAs must ensure that the child's parents are members of any group that makes decisions on the child's educational placement and, if neither parent can participate in person, other methods must be used to ensure their participation.

5. Placement decisions may be made without the involvement of parents, if the LEA cannot obtain their participation, and the LEA must have documentation of attempts to ensure their involvement.

6. LEAs must make reasonable efforts to ensure that parents understand and can participate in group discussions related to placement, including arranging for interpreters for parents with deafness or whose native language is not English.

Sec. 300.502. Independent Educational Evaluations (IEE).

1. Parents may obtain an IEE, i.e., an evaluation (a) conducted by a qualified examiner who is not employed by the agency responsible for the child's education, and (b) for which the LEA pays or ensures that it is provided at no cost to the parents.

2. LEAs must provide parents, upon request for an IEE, with information about where an IEE may be obtained and the LEA's IEE criteria.

3. Upon parents' request for an IEE at public expense, the LEA must either (a) initiate a hearing to show its evaluation is appropriate; or, (b) ensure that an IEE is provided at public expense, unless the LEA shows in a hearing that an evaluation obtained by parents did not meet LEA criteria.

4. If the LEA initiates a hearing and the hearing officer concurs that the LEA evaluation is appropriate, parents may continue with the IEE but at their own expense.

5. If parents request an IEE, the LEA may ask parents why they object to the public evaluation; however, the parents' explanation may not be required, and the LEA may not unreasonably delay either providing the IEE at public expense or initiating a hearing to defend its own evaluation.

Sec. 300.502. Independent Educational Evaluations. This provision remains the same with the following addition:

Parents are entitled to only one independent educational evaluation at public expense each time the LEA conducts an evaluation with which the parent disagrees.

6. Parents may obtain an IEE at their own expense at any time, results of which must be part of the considerations regarding provision of FAPE and may be presented as evidence at due process hearings.

7. Hearing officers may request IEEs at public expense as part of a hearing.

8. IEEs at public expense must conform to LEA criteria used in its own evaluations, including location of the evaluation and qualifications of the examiner, to the extent those criteria are consistent with parents' right to an IEE.

9. LEAs may not impose conditions or time lines beyond those in #8 on obtaining at IEE at public expense.

Sec. 300.503. Prior Notice by the Public Agency; Content of Notice.

1. Parents must be given written notice that meets the requirements (See #3 below) a reasonable time before the LEA proposes or refuses to initiate or change the identification, evaluation, educational placement, or provision of FAPE.

2. If the action in the notice also requires parental consent, the LEA may give notice at the same time consent is requested.

3. The notice must include (a) description of the action proposed or refused; (b) explanation of why

Sec. 300.503. Prior Notice by the Public Agency; Content of Notice. Provision has not changed.

the LEA proposes or refuses the action; (c) description of any other options considered and why they were rejected; (d) description of each evaluation procedure, test, record or report used as a basis for the action; (e) description of any other relevant factors; (f) statement that parents have protections under the law's procedural safeguards and, if the notice is not an initial referral for evaluation, how the procedural safeguards description may be obtained; and, (g) sources of assistance for parents in understanding the law.

4. Notice must be written in language understood by the general public and provided in parents' native language or other mode of communication used, unless clearly not feasible. If parents' native language or mode of communication is not a written language, LEAs must take step to ensure the notice is translated orally or by other means, that parents understand the notice content, and that there is a written record that these requirements have been met.

Sec. 300.504. Procedural Safeguards Notice.

1. A copy of the procedural safeguards must be given to parents, at a minimum, at initial referral for evaluation, at each notification of an

Sec. 300.504. Procedural Safeguards Notice. Changes and additions are as follows:

1. A copy of the procedural safeguards must be given to parents only one time in a school,

1999 Regulations	2006 Regulations
IEP meeting, at reevaluation, and when complaints are filed.	except that a copy must also be given at:
2. The notice must include a full explanation of the procedural safeguards and the State complaint procedures, written in native language, if feasible, and in easily understandable language.	a. Initial referral or parental request for evaluation; b. Upon receipt of the first State complaint and receipt of the first due process complaint; c. According to procedures under the discipline provisions; and
3. The notice covers regulations related to independent evaluation; prior written notice; parental consent; access to educational records; opportunity to present complaints; child's placement during due process proceedings; procedures for a child in an interim alternative educational setting; requirements for placement of the child by parents in a private school at public expense; mediation; due process hearings; appeals; civil actions; attorneys' fees; and, the State complaint procedures, including how to file and the timelines for filing.	d. At the parent's request. 2. LEAs may post the procedural safeguards notice on their Web site. 3. Additions to notice contents are as follows: a. The opportunity to present resolve complaints through the due process and State complaint procedures, including (1) time lines for filing complaints; (2) the opportunity for the agency to resolve the complaint; and, (3) the difference between the two procedures, including what issues can be raised, time lines for filing and decisions, and relevant procedures. b. Time lines for filing civil actions.

Electronic Mail. No comparable language.	*Sec. 300.505. Electronic Mail.* If the LEA provides the option, parents may choose to receive prior written notices, procedural safeguards notices, and due process complaint notices (Secs. 300.503; 300.504; 300.508) by email.

Sec. 300.506. Mediation.

1. The LEA must have mediation procedures for resolution of disputes that must be available, at a minimum, whenever a due process hearing or hearing under the discipline provisions is requested.

2. The process must be voluntary, may not be used to deny or delay parents' right to a hearing or other rights under the law, and must be conducted by a qualified impartial mediator.

3. States must maintain a list of qualified mediators who are knowledgeable in special education laws and regulations

4. If mediators are not selected on a random basis from the State list, both parties must be involved in and agree to the selection of the mediator.

5. States bear the cost of mediation.

6. Mediation sessions must be scheduled in a timely manner and held in a convenient location for both parties.

7. Agreements must be put in a written agreement.

8. Mediation discussions are confidential; parties may be required to sign a confidentiality pledge; and, discussions may not be used as evidence in subsequent hearings or civil proceedings.

Sec. 300.506. Mediation. Procedures are basically the same, with the following changes:

1. Mediation also may be used for disputes about issues arising before filing of a due process complaint.

2. For parties that opt not to use mediation, the LEA may *afford an opportunity* to meet with a disinterested party to encourage the use and explain the benefits of mediation.

3. The SEA must select mediators on a random, rotational, or other impartial basis.

4. If the dispute is resolved through mediation, a legally binding agreement, enforceable in State or federal district court, must be executed and signed by parents and an authorized agency representative.

Note: The requirement of a confidentiality pledge has been removed.

9. Mediators may not be employees of any LEA or SEA responsible for the education of the child and must not have a personal or professional conflict of interest. Persons qualified as mediators are not employees of the LEA or SEA solely because they are paid by the agency to serve as a mediator.

10. The LEA or SEA may require parents who do not choose mediation to meet with a disinterested party to urge the use and explain the benefits of mediation.

11. The right to a due process hearing may not be denied or delayed for parents' failure to participate in a meeting under #10 above.

Sec. 300.507. Impartial Due Process Hearing; Parent Notice.

1. A parent or a public agency may initiate a hearing regarding the agency's proposal or refusal to initiate or change the child's identification, evaluation, educational placement, or provision of FAPE.

2. When a hearing is requested, the LEA must inform parents of the availability of mediation.

3. LEAs must inform parents of any free or low-cost legal and other relevant services, if the parents request the information or parents or the LEA initiates a hearing.

Sec. 300.507. Filing a Due Process Complaint. New regulations add:

1. The complaint must allege a violation that occurred not more than 2 years before the party knew or should have known about the alleged action in the complaint, or if the State already has a time limitation for filing complaints, within that time frame.

2. LEAs must provide information about legal or other services if parents or the LEA "files a due process complaint" (See Sec. 300.508).

4. LEAs must have procedures requiring parents or their attorney to provide notice (which remains confidential) in a request for a hearing, which must include (a) child's name, address of residence, and school; (b) description of the problem and related facts; and, (c) proposed resolution to the extent known and available at the time.

5. SEAs must develop a model form to assist parents in filing due process requests.

6. Public agencies may not deny or delay parents' right to a due process hearing for failure to provide the notice in #5 above.

Due Process Complaint. No comparable language, but see Sec. 300.507 above and note to this section.

Sec. 300.508. Due Process Complaint.

1. Either party, or the attorney representing the party, must provide the due process complaint to the other party and must forward a copy to the SEA.

2. Complaint notice contents are the same as the notice requirements in previous regulations, Sec. 300.507. In addition, if the complaint involves a homeless child, the notice must include available contact information and the school the child is attending.

3. Notice Requirement: A party may not have a hearing on a due process complaint unless the party, or the party's attorney, files the due process complaint notice.

4. Sufficiency of the Complaint: The due process complaint is deemed sufficient unless the receiving party gives written notification to the other party and the hearing officer, within 15 days of receipt of the complaint, that the receiving party believes the complaint does not meet the requirements of this section.

   a. Within 5 days of receipt of this notification, the hearing officer must make a determination on the sufficiency of the complaint and immediately notify the parties in writing of that determination.

   b. A party may amend a complaint notice only if (1) the other party gives written consent to an amendment and has an opportunity to resolve the complaint through a resolution meeting (Sec. 300.510); or, (2) the hearing officer grants permission to amend not later than 5 days before the due process hearing begins.

   c. If a party files an amended complaint, the time lines for the resolution process (Sec. 300.510) begin again when the amended complaint is filed.

5. LEA Response to the Complaint: If the LEA has not sent prior written notice (Sec. 300.503) to the parents regarding the subject of the parent's complaint, the LEA must, within 10 days of receipt of the complaint,

send a response to the parents, including:

a. Why the LEA proposed or refused to take the action raised in complaint;

b. Other options considered and why they were rejected;

c. A description of each evaluation procedure, assessment, or record used by the LEA agency as the basis for action; and,

d. Other relevant factors.

This response does not preclude the LEA from asserting that the parents' complaint was insufficient.

6. Other Party Response: The party receiving the complaint must, within 10 days of its receipt, send a response to the other party that specifically addresses the issues raised in the complaint.

Due Process Complaint. The law now establishes that both parents and local school districts may file complaints. Previous regulations stated that "a parent or a public agency may initiate a hearing" (34 CFR Sec. 300.507); however, the statutory language was not as clear. This section establishes a new notice requirement, with information contained in the previous parent notice (Sec. 300.507), and must be filed by the complaining party. Also, the law includes a statute of limitations for filing complaints. The previous law did not limit the amount of time that could elapse between the alleged violation and bringing a complaint. This sometimes resulted in complaints being raised that allegedly occurred a number of years earlier, making fact finding more difficult and possibly resulting in orders for compensatory education long after the violation had been cured or the student had exited the school system. The statute of limitations may also serve to reduce the number of hearings and encourage attempts to resolve complaints outside the hearing process through mediation or other alternative dispute resolution mechanisms.

1999 Regulations (IDEA '97, P.L. 105-17)	2006 Regulations (IDEA '04, P.L. 108-446)
Sec. 300.507. Impartial Due Process Hearing; Parent Notice. SEAs must develop model forms to assist parents in filing due process requests.	**Sec. 300.509. Model Forms.** Additions include: 1. SEAs must develop model forms to assist parents and LEAs in filing due process complaints and parents and other parties in filing State complaints. 2. SEAs or LEAs may not require the use of model forms. 3. Other forms may be used, so long as they meet the appropriate content requirements.
Resolution Process. No comparable language.	**Sec. 300.510. Resolution Process.** 1. Within 15 days of receipt of the parents' due process complaint and before the initiation of a hearing, the LEA must call a meeting with parents and relevant IEP team members, determined by parents and the LEA, who have specific knowledge of the facts in the complaint. 2. An LEA representative with decision-making authority must attend, and the LEA's attorney may not attend unless the parent also has an attorney present. 3. The purpose of the meeting is for parents to discuss the complaint, so that the LEA has an opportunity to resolve the issues. 4. The parents and the LEA may agree in writing to waive this meeting or to use the mediation process.

5. If the LEA has not resolved the complaint to the parents' satisfaction within 30 days of its receipt, a hearing may occur.

6. Time lines for a final hearing decision begin at the end of the 30-day period, except that the 45-day hearing time line (Sec. 300.515) begins the day after one of the following:
   a. The parties agree in writing to waive the resolution meeting;
   b. After either mediation or the resolution meeting starts but prior to the end of the 30-day period, the parties agree in writing that no agreement is possible; or,
   c. If the parties agree in writing to continue mediation at the end of the 30-day resolution period, but later, one party withdraws from mediation.

7. Unless the parties have agreed to waive this process or use mediation, the parents' failure to participate in the resolution meeting will delay the time lines of the resolution and hearing processes until the meeting is held.

8. If the LEA fails to hold the meeting within the time line or fails to participate in the meeting, parents may ask a hearing officer to intervene to start the hearing time line.

9. If resolution is reached, the parties must execute and sign a legally binding agreement, which is

enforceable in State or federal district court and which may be voided by either party within 3 business days of its execution.

Resolution Process. In 1997, Congress added the option of mediation. The resolution process is another step toward attempting to resolve disagreements in a more informal and less adversarial setting than a due process hearing. Some parents had expressed concern that this process might be used to delay their right to a due process hearing. The regulations should address these concerns through clarification that the parties do not have to continue the resolution process if they agree that no agreement is possible and that each party has specific recourse if the other party fails to participate in the process.

Secs. 300.507; 300.508. Impartial Due Process Hearing; Impartial Hearing Officer.

1. Whenever a parent files a due process complaint or a request for a hearing under the discipline provisions, they must have the opportunity for an impartial due process hearing conducted by the SEA or LEA directly responsible for the child's education, as determined by State law, regulation, or policy.

2. Hearings may not be conducted by individuals who are employees of the SEA or LEA involved in the care or education of the child or who have a personal or professional interest that would conflict with their objectivity.

3. Persons qualified as hearing officers are not employees of the LEA or SEA solely because they are paid by the agency to serve as such.

Sec. 300.511. Impartial Due Process Hearing. New regulations add:

1. The party requesting a hearing may not raise issues at the hearing that were not raised in the complaint, unless the other party agrees.

2. A hearing must be requested within 2 years, or within an existing State time frame, of the date the party knew or should have known about the alleged action in the complaint.

3. The time line does not apply to parents if they were prevented from filing a complaint due to (a) specific misrepresentations by the LEA that it had resolved the complaint; or, (b) the LEA's withholding of information that was required to be provided to the parents.

4. Hearing officers must have knowledge of and the ability to (a) understand the IDEA, federal

1999 Regulations (IDEA '97, P.L. 105-17)	2006 Regulations (IDEA '04, P.L. 108-446)
4. Each public agency must keep a list of persons who serve as hearing officers, including a statement of each person's qualifications.	and State regulations, and federal and State case law interpreting the law; and, (b) conduct hearings and render and write decisions according to accepted legal practice.

Sec. 300.509. Hearing Rights.

1. Parties to a hearing have the right to (a) be accompanied and advised by counsel and by persons with special knowledge or training regarding children with disabilities; (b) present evidence and confront, cross-examine, and compel attendance of witnesses; (c) prohibit introduction of evidence at the hearing that was not disclosed at least 5 business days prior to the hearing; and, (d) have a written, or at the parents' option, electronic, verbatim hearing record and findings of fact and decisions.

2. At least 5 business days before a hearing, parties must disclose all evaluations completed by that date and recommendations they intend to bring at the hearing. If a party does not comply with disclosure, the hearing officer may bar introduction of the evaluation or recommendation without the other party's consent.

3. Parents must have the right to (a) have the child present at the hearing; and (b) open the hearing to the public.

Sec. 300.512. Hearing Rights. Provision has not changed.

4. Hearing records and findings of fact and decisions must be provided at no cost to parents.	

Hearing Decisions. No comparable language, except:
 	
Findings and decisions must be sent to the State advisory panel and be available to the public. (Sec. 300.509)
	Sec. 300.513. Hearing Decisions.
	
	1. A hearing officer's decision of whether a child received FAPE must be based on substantive grounds. If complaints allege procedural violations, the hearing officer may find that child was denied FAPE only if the alleged procedural violations:
	  a. Impeded the child's right to FAPE;
	  b. Significantly impeded the parent's opportunity to participate in the process regarding provision of FAPE; or,
	  c. Deprived the child of educational benefit.
	
	2. Parents may not be precluded from an appeal of a hearing decision to the SEA, if a State appeal process is available.
	
	3. Parents may not be precluded from filing a separate complaint on an issue separate from a complaint already filed.

Hearing Decisions. This section clarifies that complaints based solely on procedural violations will be successful only if those violations are significant. This addition addresses a continuing concern that the IDEA has focused too much on process and not enough on improving educational outcomes for students with disabilities. Requiring that the basis of complaints will be on substantive, rather than procedural, grounds reinforces the focus on results.

Sec. 300.510. Finality of Decision; Appeal; Impartial Review.

1. Hearing decisions are final, except that parties may appeal the decision.

2. If an agency other than the SEA conducts a due process hearing, parties may appeal to the SEA.

3. If there is an appeal, the SEA must conduct an impartial review, and the official conducting the review must (a) examine the hearing record; (b) ensure that due process procedures were followed; (c) ask for additional evidence if necessary; (d) give parties a chance for oral or written argument, or both, at the official's discretion; (d) make an independent decision based on the review; and, (e) give a copy of the written, or at parents' option, electronic finding of fact and decisions to the parties.

4. Findings and decisions must be sent to the State advisory panel and made available to the public.

5. The official's decision is final, unless a party brings a civil action.

Sec. 300.514. Finality of Decision; Appeal; Impartial Review.
Provision has not changed.

Sec. 300.511. Timelines and Convenience of Hearings and Reviews.

1. The LEA must ensure that, not later than 45 days after request for a due process hearing, (a) a final decision is reached; and, (b) a copy of the decision is mailed to the parties.

Sec. 300.515. Timelines and Convenience of Hearings and Reviews.
#1 changes, as follows, with the remainder the same:

"The public agency must ensure that not later than 45 days after the expiration of the 30-day period (SEA

2. The SEA must ensure that, not later than 30 days after request for a review of a hearing decision, (a) a final decision is reached; and, (b) a copy of the decision is mailed to the parties.	review), or the adjusted time periods (hearing extensions), a final decision is reached in the hearing. . . ."
3. Hearing or reviewing officers may grant specific time extensions at the request of either party.	
4. Hearings and reviews involving oral arguments must be held at a time and place reasonably convenient to the parents and child.	

Sec. 300.512. Civil Action.	**Sec. 300.516. Civil Action.** New regulations add:
1. Any party may appeal a decision in a civil action in a State or federal district court, where the State does not have an appeal process or a party wishes to appeal a State review decision.	A party has 90 days from the date of the hearing decision or the State appeal decision, or the time allowed under an existing State time line, to bring a civil action.
2. The court must receive administrative hearing records, hear additional evidence at a party's request, and, basing its decision on the preponderance of evidence, grant appropriate relief as the court determines.	
3. Before seeking a civil action, avenues of relief under the due process procedures must first be exhausted.	

1999 Regulations (IDEA '97, P.L. 105-17)	2006 Regulations (IDEA '04, P.L. 108-446)

Sec. 300.513. Attorneys' Fees.

1. At the court's discretion, reasonable attorneys' fees may be awarded to parents who are the prevailing party.

2. Part B funds may not be used to pay attorneys' fees or a party's costs related to the proceeding; however, LEAs are not precluded from using Part B funds to conduct the proceeding.

3. Fees awarded are based on prevailing community rates, and no bonus or multiplier may be used in the calculation.

4. Fees may not be awarded or related costs reimbursed for services performed after a written offer of settlement if (a) the offer is made within the Federal Rules of Civil Procedure, or, in an administrative proceeding, at any time more than 10 days before the proceeding began; (b) the offer is not accepted within 10 days; or, (c) the court or hearing officer finds the relief finally obtained by parents is not more favorable to them than the settlement offer.

5. Fees may be awarded to parents who are the prevailing party and were substantially justified in rejected the settlement offer.

6. Fees may not awarded relating to IEP team meetings, unless convened as a result of an administrative proceeding or court

Sec. 300.517. Attorneys' Fees. New regulations add:

1. Attorneys' fees may also be awarded to:
   a. A prevailing SEA or LEA against a parent's attorney (1) who files a complaint or action that is frivolous, unreasonable, or without foundation; or, (2) who continues to litigate after the litigation clearly became frivolous, unreasonable, or without foundation.
   b. A prevailing SEA or LEA against a parent's attorney or against the parent, if a complaint or subsequent action was presented for "any improper purpose," e.g., to harass, cause unnecessary delay, or needlessly increase the cost of litigation.

2. Attorneys' fees are not available for resolution meetings (Sec. 300.510).

3. Fees may be reduced if the parent or the parent's attorney unreasonably protracted the final resolution of the controversy.

action, or, at the State's discretion, for mediation prior to filing a due process request.

7. Fees may be reduced if (a) the parents unreasonably protracted the final resolution of the controversy; (b) the amount of the fees unreasonably exceeded the prevailing hourly rate that community; (c) time spent and legal services furnished were excessive; or, (d) the parents' attorney did not provide the appropriate information to the LEA (See Sec. 300.507).

8. The provisions of #7 above do not apply if the court finds that the SEA or LEA unreasonably protracted the final resolution or violated the procedural safeguards.

Attorneys' Fees. Awards of attorneys' fees under certain circumstances are now available to a school district that is a prevailing party. Award of attorneys' fees to the school district under the stated circumstances comports with provisions under other civil rights laws.

Sec. 300.514. Child's Status During Proceedings.

1. During the pendency of administrative or judicial proceedings on a due process complaint (except under the discipline provisions), the child remains in the current educational placement, unless the parents and LEA agree otherwise.

2. If the complaint involves an application for initial school

Sec. 300.518. Child's Status During Proceedings. New regulations add:

If the complaint involves an application for initial services for a child moving from Part C to Part B and the child has turned three, the LEA is not required to provide the Part C services that the child has been receiving. If the child is deemed eligible for special education and related services, the child must receive those services that are not in admission, the child, with the parents' consent, is placed in the school until proceedings are completed.

3. If the decision of a hearing officer in a hearing conducted by the SEA or the decision of a State review official agrees with the parents that a change of placement is appropriate, that placement must be treated as an agreement between the SEA or LEA and the parents for purposes of #1 above.

dispute, if the parent consents to provision of services.

Sec. 300.515. Surrogate Parents.

1. LEAs must ensure that a child's rights are protected if the parent cannot be identified or located or the child is a ward of the State.

2. The LEA's duty includes assignment of a person to act as surrogate for the parents, including methods for determining whether the child needs a surrogate parent and for assigning a surrogate.

3. Surrogate parents may be selected in any way State law permits.

4. LEAs must ensure that persons selected as surrogates (a) are not employees of the SEA, LEA, or other agency involved in the child's care or education; (b) do not have a conflict of interest; and, (c) have knowledge and skills to ensure adequate representation of the child.

Sec. 300.519. Surrogate Parents. New regulations add:

1. A surrogate must be assigned for children who are "unaccompanied homeless youth." Until a surrogate parent is appointed, a staff member of an emergency or transitional shelter or other outreach program may serve as a temporary surrogate.

2. For wards of the State, the judge may appoint the surrogate.

3. The SEA must make reasonable efforts to ensure that a surrogate parent is assigned not more than 30 days after determining the need.

112

5. Individuals who are employees of nonpublic agencies that only provide non-educational care for the child and who meet the other standards as outlined above may be assigned as surrogates.

6. Persons who otherwise qualify to be surrogates are not employees of the agency solely because they are paid by the agency to serve as surrogates.

7. Surrogates may represent children in all matters related to the identification, evaluation, educational placement, and provision if FAPE.

Sec. 300.517. Transfer of Parental Rights at Age of Majority.

1. States may provide that, when children with disabilities reach the State's age of majority that applies to all children (except for children with disabilities who have been determined incompetent under State law), (a) LEAs must provide any notices required under the IDEA to both the child and the parents, and all other rights under the IDEA accorded to the parents transfer to the child; (b) all IDEA rights accorded to parents transfer to students incarcerated in adult or juvenile State or local corrections facilities; (c) when rights are transferred, parents and the child must be notified.

Sec. 300.520. Transfer of Parental Rights at Age of Majority. Provision has not changed.

2. If State law provides a mechanism to determine that a child with a disability, who has reached the State age of majority and has not been determined incompetent under State law, does not have the ability to provide informed consent for educational decisions, the State must have procedures to appoint the parent, or, if the parent is not available, another appropriate person, to represent the child's educational interests until termination of eligibility.

Discipline Procedures	Discipline Procedures

Sec. 300.121. FAPE for Children Suspended or Expelled from School. Sec. 300.519. Authority of School Personnel; Sec. 300.523. Manifestation Determination Review.
 	
1. General Authority:
  a. To the extent applied to non-disabled children, a child may be removed from the current placement for not more then 10 consecutive school days for violations of school rules and for additional removals of not more than 10 consecutive school days during the school year for other incidents, as long as the removals do not constitute a change in placement.
  b. A child may be removed to an interim alternative educational setting (IAES) for not more than 45 days for violations involving weapons or drugs.
	Sec. 300.530. Authority of School Personnel. Changes and additions include:
	
	1. Case-by-Case Determination: School personnel may consider unique circumstances on a case-by-case basis when deciding whether to order a change in placement for a child that violates the code of student conduct.
	
	2. General Authority: To the extent applied to nondisabled children, a child who violates the code of student conduct may be removed from the current placement *to an appropriate IAES, another setting, or suspension* for not more than 10 school days and for additional removals of not more than 10 consecutive school days during

c. The LEA must (a) conduct a functional behavioral assessment (FBA) and develop a behavioral intervention plan (BIP) or review an existing plan not later than 10 business days after either first removing the child for more than 10 school days in the school year or a removal that constitutes a change in placement; and, (b) as soon as possible after developing the plan and completing the FBA, convene an IEP meeting to develop appropriate behavioral interventions.

d. If a child with a BIP is subsequently removed again, the IEP team must review the BIP, and if determined necessary, modify the plan.

2. Services: Services must be provided after removal for more than 10 school days in the same school year. However, services must only be provided to a child who has been removed from the current placement for 10 school days or less in that school year if nondisabled children receive services in the same circumstances.

a. For a child who has been removed for than 10 school days in that school year, during subsequent removals the LEA must provide services to the extent necessary for the child to progress in the general curriculum and advance toward

the school year for other incidents, as long as the removals do not constitute a change in placement.

3. Additional Authority: For changes in placement exceeding 10 school days for behavior that is not a manifestation of the disability, the same disciplinary action applicable to nondisabled children may be applied "in the same manner and for the same duration."

4. Services: Whether or not the behavior is a manifestation of the child's disability, a child removed from current placement must continue to receive educational services enabling progress toward IEP goals and participation in the general education curriculum, and receive, as appropriate, an FBA and behavioral intervention services and modifications.

a. After a child is removed for 10 school days in the same school year and the current removal is for not more than 10 consecutive school days and is not a change of placement, school personnel, in consultation with *at least one of the child's teachers,* determine the extent to which services are needed for the child to continue to participate in the general education curriculum and progress toward IEP goals.

meeting IEP goals (1)as long as the removal is not a change in placement; or, (2) the behavior was not a manifestation of the child's disability.

b. The extent of services to be provided is determined (1) by school personnel, in consultation with the child's special education teacher, for children removed for not more than 10 consecutive school days where the removal is not a change in placement; and, (2) by the child's IEP team if the child is removed for behavior that is not a manifestation of the child's disability.

3. Manifestation Determination:
   a. Not later than 10 school days after decisions on 45-day IAES placements, removals due to possible injury to the child or others, or removals constituting change in placement, the IEP team and other qualified personnel must determine whether there is a relationship between the disability and the behavior.
   b. The team and other qualified personnel may determine that the behavior was not a manifestation of the disability only if the team considers all relevant information and determines that (1) the placement and the IEP were appropriate; (2) the disability did

b. If the removal is a change of placement, the IEP team determines appropriate services.

5. Manifestation Determination:
   a. Except for short-term removals, within 10 school days of a decision to change the child's placement, the LEA, parents, and relevant IEP team members (as determined by the LEA and parents) must review all relevant information (including IEP, teacher observations and relevant information provided by parents) to determine if the conduct was (1) "caused by, or had a direct and substantial relationship to" child's disability; or, (2) was the "direct result of the LEA's failure to implement the IEP."
   b. If either instance applies, the conduct is a manifestation of the disability.
   c. If the determination is that the IEP was not implemented, the LEA must take immediate steps to remedy the deficiencies.
   d. If the conduct is determined to be a manifestation of the child's disability, the IEP team must (1) either conduct an FBA, if it was not done prior to incident, and implement a BIP or review the previous plan for modification, as needed; and, (2) except where violations involve weapons, drugs, or serious

not impair the child's ability to understand the impact and consequences of behavior; and, (3) the disability did not impair the child's ability to control the behavior.

c. If the behavior is not a manifestation of the disability, the child may be disciplined under the general conduct code.

d. If the parents disagree with the determination, they may request and will receive an expedited hearing.

bodily injury, return the child to the previous placement, unless the parents and the LEA agree to a change in placement as part of modification of the BIP.

e. School personnel may remove a child to an IAES for not more than 45 school days *without regard to whether the behavior is determined to be a manifestation of the child's disability,* in cases of violations related to drugs, weapons, or *infliction of serious bodily injury.*

Sec. 300.522(a). Determination of Setting. The IEP team determines the interim alternative educational setting for services for children removed for not more than 45 days for weapons and drugs violations.

Sec. 300.531. Determination of Setting. The IEP team determines the IAES for (a) a change in placement that would exceed 10 consecutive school days, where the behavior is not a manifesta-tion of the disability; (b) a change in placement, in accord with Sec. 300.536; and, (c) for children removed for violations involving weapons, drugs, or serious bodily injury.

Sec. 300.521. Authority of Hearing Officer; Sec. 300.528. Expedited Due Process Hearings.

1. Authority of Hearing Officer: A hearing officer may order a change in placement to an IAES for not more than 45 days if, in an expedited hearing, the hearing officer (a) determines that the LEA has shown by substantial evidence that keeping the child in the current placement is substantially likely to

Sec. 300.532. Appeal. Changes and additions are as follows:

1. Parents who disagree with placement or the manifestation determination or LEAs that believe maintaining the current placement is substantially likely to result in injury to the child or others may appeal those decisions by requesting an expedited due process hearing.

result in injury to the child or others; (b) considers the appropriateness of the current placement; (c) considers whether the LEA has made reasonable efforts to minimize the risk of harm in the current placement; and (d) determines that the proposed IAES meets the requirements of the law.

2. Expedited Due Process Hearings:
   a. An expedited due process hearing must meet all requirements of a regular due process hearing, except that the SEA may establish a shorter time line for disclosure of evidence.
   b. SEAs must establish time lines for expedited hearings that provide for a written decision mailed to the parties within 45 days of the LEA's receipt of request for a hearing, with no exceptions or extensions.
   c. SEAs may have different procedural rules for expedited hearings; however, decisions are appealable, as with regular hearings.

2. Authority of Hearing Officer:
   a. In deciding an appeal, the hearing officer may (1) return the child to the current placement if the hearing officer determines that the removal was a violation of school personnel's authority (Sec. 300.530) or that the behavior was a manifestation of the child's disability; or (2) order a change in placement to an IAES for not more than 45 days if the hearing officer determines that maintaining the child in the current placement is substantially likely to result in injury to the child or others.
   b. Appeal procedures may be repeated, if the LEA believes that returning the child to the current placement is substantially likely to result in injury to the child or others.

3. Expedited Due Process Hearing:
   a. The SEA or LEA must arrange an expedited hearing within 20 school days of the date the hearing request is filed, and a decision must be rendered within 10 school days after the hearing is held.
   b. Unless parents and the LEA agree in writing to waive the resolution meeting (Sec 300.510) or agree to use mediation, (1) a resolution meeting must be held within 7 days of receiving notice of the complaint; and (2) the hearing

may proceed unless the matter has been resolved to the satisfaction of both parties within 15 days of receipt of the complaint.

Sec. 300. 526. Placement During Appeals.

1. If parents request a hearing or an appeal of a disciplinary action to challenge the IAES or the manifestation determination, the child must remain in the IAES pending the hearing officer's decision or the expiration of the 45-day time period, whichever occurs first, unless parents and the SEA or LEA agree otherwise.

2. If a child is placed in an IAES and school personnel propose to change the child's placement after expiration of the interim alternative placement, during the pending of any challenge to the proposed change in placement, the child must remain the child's current placement, i.e., the placement prior to the IAES, except as provided in #3 below.

3. If school personnel maintain that it is dangerous for the child to be in the current placement, i.e., placement prior to the IAES, during pendency of any due process proceedings, the LEA may request an expedited hearing. The hearing officer's decision to maintain the IAES placement or order another

Sec. 300.533. Placement During Appeals. #1 remains. Some of the rest of this provision has been moved to and is reflected in Sec. 300.532.

placement must be based on the rules related to "authority of the hearing officer" (Sec. 300.521); the placement may not be longer than 45 days; and, the expedited hearing procedure may be repeated as often as necessary.

Sec. 300.527. Protections for Children Not Yet Eligible for Special Education and Related Services.

1. A child not yet determined eligible for special education and related services who violates the conduct code may assert protections of IDEA if LEA had "knowledge" that the child was "child with a disability" before the incident occurred.

2. An LEA is deemed to have "knowledge" if (a) parents expressed concern in writing to appropriate LEA personnel that the child is in need of special education; (b) the child's behavior or performance demonstrates need for services; (c) parents requested an evaluation; or, (d) the child's teacher or other school personnel expressed concern about the child's behavior or performance to the special education director or other school personnel.

3. An LEA would not be deemed to have "knowledge" if the LEA either (a) conducted an previous evaluation resulting in a determination that the child was not a child with a

Sec. 300.534. Protections for Children Not Determined Eligible for Special Education and Related Services. New regulations include the following changes:

1. LEAs are deemed to have knowledge that child is a child with a disability if (a) parents expressed concern in writing to *supervisory or administrative* personnel or *a teacher of the child* that the child needs services; or, (b) the teacher or other LEA personnel expressed "specific concerns about a pattern of behavior demonstrated by the child directly" to the special education director or other "supervisory" personnel.

2. LEAs are not deemed to have knowledge if (a) the parents have not allowed an evaluation; (b) have refused services; or, (c) the child has been evaluated and was determined not to be eligible for services.

disability; or (b) determined an
evaluation was not necessary; and,
(c) notified the parents of the
determination under (a) or (b).

Sec. 300.529. Referral to and Action by Law Enforcement and Judicial Authorities.

1. The law does not prohibit an agency from reporting crimes committed by children with disabilities to appropriate authorities or preventing State law enforcement and judicial authorities from exercising their responsibilities regarding application of State and federal law to those crimes.

2. Agencies reporting such crimes must ensure that copies of special education and disciplinary records are sent for consideration by authorities to whom crimes are reported.

3. Records may be transmitted only to the extent allowed by the Family Educational Rights and Privacy Act (FERPA).

Sec. 300.535. Referral to and Action by Law Enforcement and Judicial Authorities. Provision has not changed.

Sec. 300.519. Change of Placement for Disciplinary Removals. For purposes of removals from the child's current placement under the disciplinary provisions, a change of placement occurs if (a) the removal is for more than 10 consecutive school days; or (b) the child is subjected to a series of removals constituting a

Sec. 300.536. Change of Placement Because of Disciplinary Removals. New regulations add:

1. A change of placement also occurs if the child has been subjected to a series of removals constituting a pattern because the behavior is substantially similar to the child's

1999 Regulations (IDEA '97, P.L. 105-17)	2006 Regulations (IDEA '04, P.L. 108-446)
pattern because they total more than 10 school days in a school year and due to factors such as the length of each removal, the total amount of time the child is removed, and the proximity of the removals to each other.	behavior in previous incidents that resulted in a series of removals. 2. The LEA determines on a case-by-case basis if a pattern of removals constitutes a change of placement.
State Enforcement Mechanisms. No comparable language.	*Sec. 300.537. State Enforcement Mechanisms.* Notwithstanding the provisions that allow for judicial enforcement of mediation or resolution meeting agreements, nothing in the law prevents SEAs from using other mechanisms to enforce those agreements, provided that the mechanisms are not mandatory and do not delay or deny a party's right to seek enforcement in State or federal district court.

Discipline Procedures. Prior to 1997, the law did not mention disciplinary actions. These provisions were, in large measure, a result of serious discussion regarding whether or not schools employ a dual system of discipline. Once it was apparent that discipline provisions would become part of the law, advocates focused on how imposing disciplinary measures would be balanced with addressing behaviors that might arise as a manifestation of the child's disability. The concern about a dual disciplinary system carried over into the discussions of the 2004 amendments, resulting in a broader use of general disciplinary measures and explicit language allowing children with disabilities to be removed for any violation of the student conduct code. For infractions resulting in 45-day removals for children with disabilities, including the addition of "serious bodily injury," removals may now extend beyond the 45-day period if longer removals are applicable to nondisabled children. Children with disabilities removed for longer than 10 school days in a school year must receive educational services and behavioral interventions. In fact, a number of States have now passed laws that require continuation of services for all children removed for disciplinary reasons. These legislative actions bolster the view of some researchers that suspension and expulsion do little to improve behavior and may, in fact, leave children farther behind who act out due to academic failure.

The manifestation determination has been considerably streamlined to ease and improve implementation. School administrators expressed frustration that the determination required considerable staff time and almost always resulted in finding some connection between the behavior and the disability. The provision now requires that the conduct was "caused by, or had a direct and substantial relationship to, the child's disability." Previously the law specifically addressed only what the school district must do when the behavior was not a manifestation of the disability. Now the law addresses what actions will be taken if the behavior is or is not a manifestation. Students may be removed to an interim alternative educational setting without a manifestation determination when the violation involves weapons, drugs, or serious bodily injury.

The House bill had eliminated the functional behavioral assessment, which was retained in the final legislation. The functional behavioral assessment involves a review of how the child functions across settings—school, home, community—and is used to develop a plan that addresses the underlying cause of the behavior.

Subpart F—Monitoring, Enforcement, Confidentiality, and Program Information

1999 Regulations (IDEA '97, P.L. 105-17)	2006 Regulations (IDEA '04, P.L. 108-446)
Monitoring, Technical Assistance, and Enforcement	**Monitoring, Technical Assistance, and Enforcement**
State Monitoring and Enforcement. No comparable language.	*Sec. 300.600. State Monitoring and Enforcement.* 1. States are required to monitor implementation of the law by LEAs 2. The primary focus of monitoring must be on improving "educational results and functional outcomes for all children with disabilities." 3. Monitoring priorities will be (a) provision of FAPE in least

1999 Regulations (IDEA '97, P.L. 105-17)	2006 Regulations (IDEA '04, P.L. 108-446)
	restrictive environment (LRE), (b) State's general supervisory authority, and (c) disproportionate representation of ethnic and racial minorities resulting in inappropriate identification.
	4. SEAs must use quantifiable indicators, qualitative indicators, as necessary, and indicators for State performance plans to measure performance on priority areas.
State Performance Plans. No comparable language.	*Sec. 300.601. State Performance Plans.* States must have a performance plan, approved by the Secretary and reviewed every 6 years by the State, to evaluate implementation efforts and describe how implementation will be improved. States must establish "measurable and rigorous targets" for indicators under priority areas, collect data, and report annually to the Secretary.
State Use of Targets and Reporting; Secretary's Review and Determination Regarding State Performance. No comparable language.	*Secs. 300.602; 300.603. State Use of Targets and Reporting; Secretary's Review and Determination Regarding State Performance.* States use targets to analyze and report annually to the public on LEAs' performance and to the Secretary on the State's performance, and the Secretary annually reviews performance plans and determines if States meet the law's requirements or need assistance to implement the law.

1999 Regulations (IDEA '97, P.L. 105-17)	2006 Regulations (IDEA '04, P.L. 108-446)
Sec. 300.587. Enforcement.	*Sec. 300.604. Enforcement; 300.605. Withholding Funds; Sec. 300.608. State Enforcement.*
1. If the Secretary finds that there has been a substantial failure by the SEA to comply with the law or failure to comply with any condition of an SEA's or LEA's eligibility, the Secretary may take the following actions: (a) withholding all or part of further payments to the State; (b) refer the matter to the Department of Justice; or (c) take any other enforcement action authorized by law.	1. Enforcement:
	a. "Needs Assistance": If, for 2 consecutive years, the Secretary determines that an SEA needs assistance in implementing the law, the Secretary does one or more of the following: (a) advises the SEA of technical assistance sources; (b) directs the use of State-level funds to where assistance is needed; or, (c) identifies the SEA as a high-risk grantee and imposes conditions on its grant.
2. If the Secretary determines that withholding funds is appropriate, the Secretary may limit the withholding to programs, projects, or portions of those affected by the failure, or that the SEA may not make further payments to certain LEAs affected by the failure.	b. "Needs Intervention": If, for 3 or more consecutive years, it is determined that an SEA needs intervention, the Secretary may take any of the actions described above and must do one or more of the following: (a) require corrective action or an improvement plan if the problem can be corrected in 1 year; (b) require a compliance agreement if the situation cannot be corrected in 1 year; (c) for each year of the determination, withhold not less than 20% or more than 50% of the SEA's funds until the problems are corrected; (d) seek to recover funds; (e) withhold some or all of payments; or, (f) refer for appropriate enforcement, including to the Department of Justice.
3. Before any funds are withheld or referrals for enforcement, notice and opportunity for a hearing must be provided to the SEA.	

c. "Needs Substantial Intervention":
The Secretary must do one
or more of the following:
(a) recover funds; (b) withhold
some or all payments; (c) refer
to the U.S. Department of
Education Inspector General; or,
(d) refer for appropriate
enforcement, including to the
Department of Justice.

2. Opportunity for Hearing: Before
withholding funds, the Secretary
must provide notice and opportunity for hearing. Pending outcome
of the hearing, payments and/or
authority to obligate funds may be
suspended.

3. State Enforcement: If an SEA finds
that an LEA is not meeting the
requirements, the SEA must
prohibit the LEA from reducing its
maintenance of effort for any year.

4. States are not restricted from using
any other authority available to
monitor and enforce the requirements of the law.

Monitoring, Technical Assistance, and Enforcement. The previous law
stated that, when a State had not substantially complied with the requirements
of the law, the Secretary could withhold payments or refer the matter for
appropriate action, including to the Department of Justice. The new law directs
federal and State monitoring to focus more heavily on improving educational
results than in the past, where the emphasis was mainly on process, and
provides for a series of sanctions for several levels of non-compliance.

Confidentiality of Information	Confidentiality of Information

Sec. 300.571. Consent.	**Sec. 300.622. Consent.** New regulations add:
1. Parental consent must be obtained before personally identifiable information is (a) disclosed to anyone other than officials of participating agencies; or (b) used for any purpose other than to meet requirements of the law.	1. Parental consent or the consent of a child who has reached the age of majority is required before personally identifiable information is released to officials of agencies providing or paying for transition services.
2. Information may not be released to participating agencies without parental consent unless authorized to do so under the Family Educational Rights and Privacy Act of 1974 (FERPA).	2. If a child is enrolled, or going to enroll, in a private school located in an LEA other than where the parents reside, parental consent is required before personally identifiable information is released between the LEA where the private school is located and the LEA of the parents' residence.

Confidentiality. This portion of the regulations—Secs. 300.610–300.627— basically track requirements on disclosure of educational records found in the Family Educational Rights and Privacy Act (FERPA). Other than the change in the Consent section noted above, these regulations have not changed.

Reports—Program Information	Reports—Program Information

Sec. 300.751. Annual Report of Children Served—Information Required; Sec. 300.755. Disproportionality.	**Sec. 300.641. Annual Report of Children Served—Information Required; Sec. 300.646. Disproportionality.** New regulations add or change:
1. Annual Report of Children Served: SEAs must report on the number of children with disabilities receiving services on December 1, or at the	1. Annual Report of Children Served (Child Count): SEAs must report on the number of children receiving

SEA's discretion on the last Friday in October.

2. Disproportionality: States must collect and examine data to determine if significant disproportionality based on race is occurring with respect to (a) identification of children with disabilities; and, (b) placement of children in particular settings.

services on any date between October 1 and December 1 of each year.

2. Disproportionality:

   a. States must also collect and examine data related to the incidence, duration, and type of disciplinary actions, including suspensions and expulsions.

   b. SEAs must require any LEA identified as having significant disproportionality (1) to reserve the maximum amount of funds under Sec. 300.226 to provide comprehensive early intervening services particularly, but not exclusively, to children in groups that were significantly overidentified; and, (2) to report to the public on revision of policies, practices, and procedures to address the problem.

Subpart G—Authorization, Allotment, Use of Funds, Authorization of Appropriations

1999 Regulations (IDEA '97, P.L. 105-17)

2006 Regulations (IDEA '04, P.L. 108-446)200

LEA High Cost Fund. No comparable language

Sec. 300.704(c). Local Educational Agency High Cost Fund. The statute and regulations include the high cost fund as a new state-level activity. For the purpose of assisting LEAs in meeting the needs of "high need children," States may opt to reserve annually 10 percent of the amount they reserve for State-level activities to establish a high cost fund. The State must establish a definition of a "high need child with a disability," eligibility criteria for participation of LEAs, and an annual schedule for disbursement of funds.

Subpart H—Preschool Grants

1999 Regulations (IDEA '97, P.L. 105-17)

2006 Regulations (IDEA '04, P.L. 108-446)

Sec. 301.1–301.32. Preschool Grants.

1. Grants are provided to States under this section to serve children with disabilities, ages 3 through 5, and, at the State's discretion, 2-year-olds turning 3 during the school year. States receiving grants must provide FAPE to children served.

2. States shall use funds reserved for State-level activities for support services, direct services, coordinated services system, and meeting State performance goals.

3. Part C does not apply to any children receiving FAPE under this section.

Sec. 300.814. Preschool Grants. State reserve funds may be used for two new activities:

1. Provision of Part C early intervention services to children eligible for preschool who previously received Part C services until they enter or are eligible for kindergarten; or,

2. At a State's discretion, to continue service coordination or case management for families receiving services under Part C.

PART C: Infants and Toddlers with Disabilities

Note: New regulations for the Infants and Toddlers program have not yet been promulgated. The Notice of Proposed Rulemaking is expected later in 2006, with new regulations anticipated in 2007. The following information reflects the 2004 statutory changes.

IDEA 1997 (P.L. 105-17)

Secs. 631–644.

1. Grants are provided to assist states to establish and maintain a coordinated, multidisciplinary, interagency system of early intervention services for infants and toddlers with disabilities and their families.

2. The Statewide system (Sec. 635) must include the following components, among others:
   a. A definition of "developmental delay."
   b. Policies ensuring services are available to all eligible infants and toddlers and their families, including Indian children residing on reservations.
   c. Comprehensive multidisciplinary evaluations of all children and identification of families' needs in assisting in their child's development.
   d. Individualized family service plans (IFSP), including service coordination, for each eligible child and family.
   e. A child find system, including referral system.

IDEA 2004 (P.L. 108-446)

Sec. 635. Requirements for Statewide System. Additions to the system include:

1. Services are based, *to the extent practicable, on scientifically based research* and available to infants/toddlers with disabilities, including *homeless children.*

2. Child find includes "rigorous standards" of identification to reduce need for future services.

3. Public awareness targets parents of premature infants or those with other physical risk factors associated with learning or developmental problems.

4. Training is provided for personnel on the social and emotional development of young children.

Sec. 635. Flexibility to Serve 3 Year Olds Until Elementary School.
The SEA and the Part C lead agency may develop a joint system allowing Part C children eligible for Preschool services to continue in Part C until they enter or eligible for kindergarten.

1. The system must ensure:
   a. Annual notice to parents of the right to receive Part B or C

f. Public awareness programs focusing on early identification.

g. A State interagency coordinating council (SICC).

h. Systems of personnel development and personnel standards.

i. Policies ensuring services are provided, to the maximum extent appropriate, in the natural environment.

2. States must submit a grant application (Sec. 637) containing, among other items:

a. Designation of the lead agency responsible for administration.

b. If a State provides services to at-risk infants and toddlers, a description of those services.

c. Policies and procedures to ensure smooth transitions from Part C to preschool or other appropriate services.

3. States must provide procedural safeguards to families, similar to Part B procedures.

4. The Federal Interagency Coordinating Council is established to minimize duplication of programs and activities across federal, State, and local agencies; ensure effective coordination of federal early intervention and preschool services across agencies; identify gaps in programs and services; and, identify barriers to interagency cooperation.

service, with an explanation of program differences, including possible costs to parents for Part C services.

b. Services, including an educational component promoting school readiness and incorporating pre-literacy, language, and numeracy skills.

c. The child may receive FAPE under Part B, if parents so choose.

d. IFSP services continue while the eligibility determination is made.

e. Informed written consent before child turns 3 is required for continuation of Part C services.

f. Substantiated cases of trauma due to exposure to family violence trigger an automatic referral for Part C services.

2. The State must report on the number and percentage of children eligible for Preschool but whose families opt to continue Part C services.

3. The State is not required to provide FAPE for preschool-aged children served under Part C.

Sec. 637. State Application and Assurances. The application includes a description of (a) policies requiring referral for children involved in substantiated cases of neglect/abuse or affected by substance abuse; and, (b) efforts to promote collaboration among Early Head Start, early education and child care programs, and Part C.

| | *Added Sec. 640(b)—Obligations Related to & Methods of Ensuring Services.* Basically the same as Part B, Sec. 612(a)(12), establishing financial responsibility for services through interagency agreements. |

Sec. 641. State Interagency Coordinating Council (Note: The Federal Interagency Coordinating Council was deleted). New SICC members include representatives of the Medicaid program, education programs for homeless children, and agencies responsible for foster care and for children's mental health.

Sec. 643(e). Reservation for State Incentive Grants. In any year when the federal appropriation for Part C exceeds $460 million, the Secretary shall reserve 15% of the increase for State grants for flexibility provisions (See Sec. 635 above).

PART D: National Activities to Improve Education of Children with Disabilities

Note: The programs in Part D of the statute are discretionary grants. Regulations on specific provisions of the Personnel Development to Improve Services and Results for Children with Disabilities are found at 34 C.F.R. 304. For the remainder, there are no accompanying regulations. Rather, priorities and additional information are contained in individual grant application announcements. Therefore, the following information reflects 2004 statutory changes.

Part D programs provide support for the Part B and Part C grant programs through research, professional development, and technical assistance. These programs have been reorganized in P.L. 108-446, although most of the same functions and activities remain. There are new focuses on coordinating grants with requirements under NCLB and on ensuring that academic achievement of children with disabilities improves as a result of these grants. Other major focuses include ensuring that programs and services are based on scientifically-based research and ensuring appropriate training for both general and special education personnel, including related services personnel and administrators, to meet the needs of children with disabilities. Several new sections in Part D are highlighted below.

IDEA 1997 (P.L. 105-17)	IDEA 2004 (P.L. 108-446)
Subpart 1. State Program Improvement Grants. These competitive grants will assist States to reform and improve educational, early intervention, and transition systems to improve student results. At least 75 percent of funds must be used to ensure sufficient numbers of personnel.	*Subpart 1. State Personnel Development Grants.* 1. In any year when the appropriation for this section is less than $100 million, competitive grants will be awarded, with priority to States with greatest personnel shortages or that demonstrate the greatest difficulty in meeting "Personnel Qualifications" requirements (Sec. 612(a)(14)). 2. In years where the appropriation equals or exceeds $100 million, formula grants will be awarded to all States. 3. State Personnel Development Plan are required, and not less than 90 percent of the grant must be used for professional development.
Accountability for Students Held to Alternative Achievement Standards. No comparable language in IDEA '97.	*Subpart 2. Sec. 664(c). Accountability for Students Held to Alternative Achievement Standards.* These national studies will examine criteria that States use in determining eligibility for alternate assessments, validity and reliability of instruments and

	procedures, alignment with State content standards, and use and effectiveness in appropriately measuring progress and outcomes specific to individualized instructional need.
Interim Alternative Educational Settings, Behavioral Supports, and Systemic School Interventions. No comparable language in IDEA '97.	*Subpart 2. Sec. 665. Interim Alternative Educational Settings, Behavioral Supports, and Systemic School Interventions.* The purpose of these grants is to support safe learning environments that foster academic achievement by improving quality of interim settings and providing increased behavioral supports and systemic interventions. Funds may support activities such as training for staff on identification, preferral and referral procedures and on positive behavioral supports and interventions and classroom management; stronger linkages between school-based and community mental health services; and use of behavioral specialists and related services personnel to implement behavioral supports. Funds may also be used to improve interim alternative educational settings by improving staff training, providing referrals for counseling services, increased use of instructional technology, and promoting interagency coordination of service delivery.

1999 Regulations (IDEA '97, P.L. 105-17)	2006 Regulations (IDEA '04, P.L. 108-446)
Subpart 2. Sec. 682. Parent Training and Information Centers. These grants are awarded to parent organizations to support centers that provide training and information to parents, particularly to underserved parents and parents of children inappropriately identified, and to assist parents to understand their rights under the law.	*Subpart 3. Sec. 671. Parent Training and Information Centers.* New required activities include: 1. Providing training and information to parents to enable their children to meet "developmental and functional goals" and challenging academic achievement goals and be prepared for independent living. 2. Providing training and information meeting needs of low-income parents and parents of limited English proficient children. 3. Helping parents participate in school activities benefiting their children. 4. Helping parents understand, prepare for, and participate in "resolution sessions" (Sec. 615(f)(1)(B)).
National Instructional Materials Access Center. No comparable language in IDEA '97.	*Subpart 3. Sec. 674(e). National Instructional Materials Access Center.* The Secretary establishes and supports the NIMAC to receive and maintain a catalogue of print instructional materials prepared in the National Instructional Materials Accessibility Standard (NIMAS), provide access to these materials, and adopt procedures to protect against copyright infringement.

1999 Regulations (IDEA '97, P.L. 105-17)	2006 Regulations (IDEA '04, P.L. 108-446)
National Center for Special Education Research. No comparable language in IDEA '97.	***Title II. National Center for Special Education Research (NCSER).*** Title II amends the Education Sciences Reform Act of 2002 (20 U.S.C. 9501 et. seq.) and becomes Part E of that Act. The Education Sciences Reform Act established the Institute, which replaces the Office of Educational Research and Information (OERI) as the main research branch of the U.S. Department of Education. Special education research previously was not housed under OERI, but is now a part of the new NCSER.
	1. The Center will carry out research activities that are consistent with its mission to:
	a. Sponsor research to expand knowledge and understanding of the needs of infants, toddlers, and children with disabilities in order to improve developmental, educational, and transitional results.
	b. Sponsor research to improve services under the law in order to improve:
	(1) Academic achievement, functional outcomes, and educational results.
	(2) Developmental outcomes for infants and toddlers with disabilities.
	c. Evaluate implementation and effectiveness of the IDEA.
	2. The Commissioner of Special Education Research will direct the Center and will propose a research

	plan to the Director of the Institute, developed in collaboration with the Assistant Secretary of Education for Special Education and Rehabilitative Services, that a. Is consistent with priorities and mission of the Institute and the Center. b. Is consistent with purposes of the IDEA. c. Has appropriate balance across all age ranges and types of disabilities. d. Provides for objective research and uses measurable indicators to assess progress and results.

Index

146

LEARNING DISABILITIES
(See specific learning disabilities)

LEAST RESTRICTIVE ENVIRONMENT (LRE)

LIMITED ENGLISH PROFICIENT

PARENTAL CONSENT (see "Consent")

PARENTALLY PLACED PRIVATE SCHOOL
CHILDREN WITH DISABILITIES

163